M CONCRETE FAITH

Wilson
Concrete
Faith

Barn
Across the Spectrum

THE INSIDE STORY OF **THE EDEN NETWORK**

A Message Trust Publication
Manchester, England, Copyright © Matt Wilson 2012

For Grace, Izaac and J.J.
– my companions on the journey

A Message Trust Publication.
The Message Trust is a registered charity (reg charity no. 1081467)
with its headquarters at
Lancaster House, Harper Road, Manchester, M22 4RG, England.
www.message.org.uk
ISBN 978-0-9571414-1-4
eISBN: 978-0-9571414-2-1
Printed and bound in England by CPI

ART DIRECTION & GRAPHIC DESIGN
Dan Hasler, Message:Creative: www.messagecreative.com

COVER PHOTO
Katy Lunsford: www.katylunsford.com

IMAGE CREDITS
All chapter images used are taken from www.flickr.com
and used under the (cc) 2.0 license.

We would like to thank the following:
    CHAPTER ONE - TenThirtyNine
    CHAPTER TWO - Missi1005
    CHAPTER THREE - TheGiantVermin
    CHAPTER FOUR - OiMax
    CHAPTER FIVE - procsilas
    CHAPTER SIX - seier+seier
    CHAPTER SEVEN - Jynto
    CHAPTER EIGHT - Lauren Manning
    CHAPTER NINE - EricFischer
    CHAPTER TEN - Lauren Manning

CONTENTS

FOREWORD

Concrete Faith is such a brilliant title and I'll tell you why!

Firstly, of course, these stories describe a faith that is contextually concrete. For more than fifteen years the Eden Network has been revealing the presence of Christ in the concrete jungles of Manchester and more recently in some of the most deprived areas of central London and other great cities. I'll never forget staying with a newly married couple who'd deliberately moved onto a particular street in Salford where almost every other house was boarded up and abandoned. Instead of greenery there was graffiti, broken windows and despair. That Eden team, like so many described in this book, was living out the good news of faith in a hard, concrete habitat.

The second reason I love the title is that Matt Wilson describes a faith that is theologically concrete, in the sense of earthed and solid. He and his mates aren't interested in discussing spiritual niceties. They are bringing the kingdom of heaven to earth in thousands of real and practical ways; allowing their hearts to be broken with the things that break the heart of God. Eden is renewing parts of the earth that hyper-spiritual Christians would damn with disgust or indifference. I remember attending a particular Eden meeting one Sunday and ripping up my colour-coded talk notes because the crowd simply wouldn't have related to the things I'd been planning to say. Instead I just perched on a bar stool and yacked and yarned, telling stories about the sorts of things I thought they might relate to. My original talk might have been fine for somewhere in the suburbs but my audience that day needed something, well, more – concrete.

Finally, I love the title of this book because it describes a faith that is concrete socially and historically. The Eden Network's success over more than fifteen years has been measurable, substantial and impressive. In an age of hype, hyperactivity and austerity, these stories of endurance and sacrifice are all the more impressive. Eden proves that the gospel can still change real lives, families and entire urban priority communities for good. They have pioneered and proven a model of urban mission that works in the twenty-first century. And behind the model there are values which are sound. And underpinning both the values and the model there is a set of deep relationships which have now endured for decades. Thanks to Eden we have a scalable, reproducible way of taking Christian faith to the concrete heartlands and making our faith concrete in those very places to the glory of God. I wish we had Eden teams on every housing estate, in every town and city in the land because I suspect that if we did, we wouldn't be far from the revivals of Wesley and Booth. Read this book, and I think you'll be inclined to agree.

Pete Greig
24-7 Prayer / Alpha International

GARDEN CITY

They will say, "This land that was laid waste has become like the garden of Eden; the cities that were lying in ruins, desolate and destroyed, are now fortified and inhabited."

Ezekiel 36:35

Our Scriptures that bring us the story of salvation ground us unrelentingly in place. Everywhere and always they insist on this grounding... "Eden, in the east" is the first place name in the Bible. It comes with the unqualified affirmation that place is good, essential, and foundational for providing the only possible creation conditions for living out our human existence truly.

Eugene Peterson

Urban contradictions

Let's try a little word-association game:

Inner City

Council Estate

I wonder what kind of images fill your mind when you hear those phrases? Foreboding concrete tower blocks? Layer after layer of graffiti? Burnt-out cars? Menacing gangs peering through their hoods? Or how about an old geezer wobbling on a ladder to water his hanging basket? Or a group of young mums sat around a corral of buggies in the brightly painted park? Or a young dad splashing his son as they wash the car together?

I hope some of the images from the bottom half of that list resonate with you as much as those from the top. I say that because this book is probably more about wrestling with contradictions than about providing comforting easy answers. Right from the outset we must embrace the fact that inner-city neighbourhoods and outer-rim estates alike can be all these things at the same time. The responsibility falls to us to choose what we will see – how we will see. That's not just about being a glass half-empty or a glass half-full person – it's about choosing to acknowledge the presence of the contradiction.

During the 2010 election the Conservatives campaigned heavily on a message of mending 'Broken Britain', so much so that cross-dressing, marathon-running comedian Eddie Izzard waded into the fray with his own party political broadcast for the Labour Party. His opinion – "Britain's not broken – it's bloody brilliant!" As Christians we ought to be able to hold the brokenness and the brilliance together in creative tension. We are, after all, those who understand that we are in the time of the in-breaking kingdom – the now but not yet.

What's the situation that this now-but-not-yet kingdom

is arriving into? In our case it's a small island with over 60 million people squeezed onto its bumpy surface. This may seem unbelievable if you live in the kind of place I grew up, where a hop over the back fence would land you in a farmer's field. Official figures show that of these 60 million, almost 90% are living within the orbit of a relatively small number of urbanised city regions. Just four of those areas together account for more than a quarter of the total UK population! The Greater London metropolis is home to a population of nearly 9 million; the West Midlands industrial heartland, encompassing Birmingham, Wolverhampton, Dudley and Walsall, houses about 2.5 million. This is mirrored in the Greater Manchester urban sprawl which swallows up huge Northern towns like Bolton, Oldham, and Stockport. Drive 45 minutes east on the M62 and you'll hit the tightly packed towns and cities of Yorkshire such as Leeds, Sheffield, Bradford, Huddersfield and Wakefield that gross their own total of nearly 2 million lives. North of the border, Glasgow and its satellites are occupied by well over 1 million residents.

Figures also show that it's within these urban areas that the vast majority of Britain's social problems reside. Urban areas are the front line of the police's fight against crime and disorder; they are where crises in the classroom and crises in the community exacerbate one other; they are where health problems abound and where life expectancy is noticeably reduced. And within the urban areas, because of their historic and systemic inequalities, there will be some neighbourhoods that are suffering disproportionately, places in which the problems are extreme, and generationally entrenched.

Given all this then, we don't have an excuse for burying our head in the sand, or for walking on the other side of the street.

Neglected Neighbourhoods

In the last 100 years Britain's urban regions have presented the church with an overwhelming missional challenge. In pretty much every city on the map, the church has failed to adapt to the changing social and cultural landscape and has been hit by major decline. But as the twentieth century turned into the twenty-first, the tide seemed to change for the church in some British cities. Hotspots of spiritual life and vitality began to appear. One of these expressions of life is the subject of this book – the Eden Network. And the story begins in a forgotten corner of Manchester, in the mid-1990s.

Manchester is often thought of as representative of UK urban dereliction and depression. Looking for a story about high crime, poor health, shoddy housing, educational underachievement, unemployment, lack of opportunity? You won't have to look far in Manchester. If you've got the courage to take a little detour away from the slick tarmac of the main arterial routes in and out of the city, you'll soon come across a neglected no-go neighbourhood, once tightly knit, now falling apart like a worn-out garment. In some quarters of the city you'll find families attempting to get to grips with life in row upon row of dated, back-to-back 'Coronation Street' housing. These are the remnants of the old Victorian slums that became a low-cost option for the waves of immigrants arriving through the latter half of the twentieth century. However, the larger proportion of the children and young people growing up in Manchester are doing so in the council estates – vast mazes of anonymous streets. The biggest of these, covering an area of about 15 square miles to the south of the city near the busy international airport, is Wythenshawe.

At its peak this estate was home to 100,000 souls, most of them rehoused during the pre- and post-war slum clearance operations. The master-planners of the period described the new community as a 'Garden City'. How apt, or perhaps ironic then, that this is where Eden would begin.

Back in 1952, my gran was certainly impressed with the brand new two-bedder she was given the keys to. The house had been built as part of the 'homes fit for heroes' drive and was a huge contrast to the cramped, damp, two-up two-down terrace in the inner city. My mum was only a baby at the time and so escaped becoming acquainted with outside privies and cobbled streets; in this new council house she'd have not just one but two gardens – front and back! One of the things my granddad was less impressed with was the long bicycle ride he faced every day in order to get to work in the giant factories of Trafford Park. Rain or shine he'd no choice but to make the journey because in the new estate, jobs and amenities were few and far between. This lack of essential economic and social organs would prove to be a major contributor toward the problems of social decay that would begin to bite hard in the following generations.

Movement with a Message

If we now know a little about where Eden began, we still need to know why. To find that out we need to time-travel to the late eighties. A young entrepreneur called Andy Hawthorne was running a business together with his brother Simon. Their accessory business was enjoying bumper orders on the back of a fashion craze kick-started by Princess Diana, who'd been photographed wearing a pair of men's elastic braces over a crisp white blouse. Operators for the production line had to be found as quickly as possible, and the qualifications for such a job were zero. This meant that the brothers found themselves with a lot of new employees who brought a barrow-load of issues into work with them. Graffiti, vandalism, fighting, theft – it was all in a day's work for these lads. Yet it was the sheer godlessness of these young lads' lives that broke Andy and Simon's hearts. Of all the deprivations to be endured by young people growing up in Longsight, it was being deprived of the opportunity of knowing a God who loved them that seemed the ultimate injustice. Shocked by these messy encounters in the factory, they turned their entrepreneurial energy toward a kingdom vision. In a burst of evangelistic innovation they shook up the city's youth culture with a series of high-profile and extremely fruitful mission events.

The momentum of these events was quickly channelled into the formation of a new ministry to take forward the brothers' vision of reaching a lost generation for Jesus. It was called The Message Trust. Andy left the business and became the Trust's director. The initiative that defined its early years was a music project that began in a bedroom and then exploded across the globe. Together with his collaborators at the time, Mark Pennells and Zarc Porter, Andy discerned a *kairos* moment in youth culture, a time of dangerous opportunity. It was 1992 and Manchester had become known by the name 'Madchester' as it was the global centre of a crazy music scene called 'rave'. All the sweaty nightclubs, all the pirate radio stations and all the boy racers in their cars with go-faster stripes were pumping out rave music 24/7. Maybe these repetitive 130bpm tunes could actually be a platform for the gospel? Rather than putting on lots more big expensive events the guys chose to focus on high schools, delivering a combination of assemblies, RE lessons and after-school concerts. The logic was that in a city with a quarter of its population under the age of 18, spending most of your time in school is a great way to get your message heard.

Andy now talks in fond but slightly mocking tones about

how the whole thing came about. You sense the genuine surprise he felt when teenagers in local schools began to go nuts as he shouted "Rub a dub dub in a big bad tub" into a microphone, whilst jumping around on the stage in an ostentatious costume, to the sound of frantic synthesisers and heavy drumbeats! The group was christened 'The World Wide Message Tribe' (aka The Tribe) and it would go on to play a huge part in Eden's genesis. With a team of energetic dancers they took their high-octane gospel show to hundreds of high schools, meeting thousands of young people and riding high on a wave of rave.

The growth of the ministry was exponential. Hundreds and hundreds of teenagers were committing their lives to Christ. Week after week The Tribe would move from school to school making the most almighty commotion. The sheer number of bookings meant hiring more team members to cope with the demanding schedule. For three or four years the whole thing was a blur – it just flew by. Andy and the team were keen to visit any high school anywhere in Greater Manchester, and they didn't want to miss anyone. However, a pattern was beginning to emerge, very subtly at first. It became noticeable that more of The Tribe's time seemed to be spent in suburban schools. Here, full-time youth pastors could support and follow up the outreach, backed up by the well-resourced churches who could make a generous donation at the end of the week toward The Tribe's ongoing work. On the surface of it this wasn't a problem – all these teenagers needed to hear about God's great love for them, whatever their postcode. And yet something didn't feel quite right – this ministry that had its original divine spark in the heart of the inner city was drifting away from the youth of the ghettoes.

Painful Birth

One place that was still on the annual schedule was Wythenshawe. At the time it had four state high schools and over a fortnight The Tribe visited the toughest two, bringing them together for a massive concert at the local Civic Forum, a concrete carbuncle with a thousand-seater auditorium. On the night of the concert the place was absolutely packed out. The Tribe were on top form and Andy preached his heart out, passionately proclaiming the pain and the power of the cross. Well over a hundred of the estate's teenagers responded to his message. In the cramped and chaotic counselling room Andy prayed with them all and then, as was the tradition, invited them along to church on Sunday. And that's when things started getting interesting.

King's Church, a small fellowship meeting every Sunday in an anteroom at the Forum Centre, had happily agreed to partner with The Message in the mission. They'd supported in every way they could: a few members of the congregation even donned the obligatory fluorescent yellow jackets and stewarded the concert, and many more had joined in praying for a breakthrough. But nobody quite expected what happened next.

It was Sunday evening and a few church members were busily setting up the PA system and organising the chairs for the special follow-up event. Astonishingly, young people started turning up – and not just in ones and twos – in great mobs! It seemed like the youth of Wythenshawe were well up for the new experience of finding out what church was all about. In total about a hundred of them showed up, bringing with them their effing and jeffing, their spliffs, their dogs and their pungent teenage aromas.

How would the little church ever cope with this lot? How could they possibly begin to disciple these wild young people? Much like the streets of the estate, the mess of their lives was plain for all to see. These were kids who weren't being loved well at home; kids carrying deep pain and confusion from the things they'd seen, heard and experienced. Unsurprisingly, over the next few weeks the teenagers started to fade away. A small handful made meaningful connections and began to grow in God, but the vast majority simply evaporated like overnight puddles on a sunny morning.

There was real heartache over seeing these broken young people, made in God's image, responding so genuinely, then disappearing again so quickly. It was too much for King's Church and The Tribe to take. This pain was channelled into a fundamental shift of mindset for all involved. Young people in the estate were desperate to know God but the existing church wasn't resourced or ready to take them on, at least not on the scale required. A revolution was needed, and there can be no revolution without revolutionaries....

The Original Pioneers

Unless he's been hiding a secret Che Guevara fantasy from me all these years I'm pretty sure that Dave Nuttall isn't in the habit of wearing camouflage fatigues. Despite that, and although he may be reluctant to admit it, he is a true revolutionary. On the 9th October 1996, Dave became the first person to move into an 'Eden project'. At the time the Benchill area of Wythenshawe was officially the most deprived ward in the whole of the UK. Once an acclaimed model of post-war town planning, it had become notorious throughout the Manchester region for its volatile mix of drug dealing, burglary and social breakdown.

Now well into his second decade in Benchill, Dave recalls exactly what he brought with him as he embarked on his new life in the 'hood:

"I had a teaspoon, a knife and fork, a mug, a plate, a kettle, a loaf of bread, a jar of peanut butter, a jar of coffee, a bag of sugar, four pints of milk, a huge fridge-freezer – empty apart from the milk – a five-foot fold-out camp bed, a pillow, a duvet, a radio alarm clock, a wooden fold-up chair, and the clothes I stood up in."

This list shouldn't be misunderstood. It doesn't describe Dave's commitment to living an austere monastic lifestyle. And he wasn't travelling light just in case he had to beat a hasty retreat back to the suburbs either. A few weeks prior to his moving-in date, Dave's mum had bought a new lawnmower. It had arrived in a big sturdy cardboard box. Day by day Dave had been neatly packing all his worldly goods into that box, all the personal things that defined him, his favourite books and videos, his treasured Beatles albums. All safely stacked in the lawnmower box.

Not having his own car, Dave had arranged a bit of help to get him and his lawnmower box the five miles down the road to Wythenshawe. Just as the sky was turning to dusk he heard the gentle pip of the horn and knew it was time to make his move. Bending his knees and wrapping his arms around the box bear-hug style he counted down to the clean and jerk, "3... 2... 1... LIFT!" And then time froze as the base of the box, with no respect for time or occasion, ripped open, emptying its precious contents all over Dave's feet like a tourist with a nasty case of Delhi Belly. Deflated, frustrated and feeling the pressure of needing to arrive and unload before dark, a quick whiz round the house was all there was time for. In true Matthew 10 style, Dave would be travelling light.

Moving into Benchill and becoming founder member of the new Eden team there was not entirely a leap into the unknown for Dave. For a year his fiancée Colette Vickers, a trainee physiotherapist and dancer with The Tribe, had sensed God speaking to her about his dreams for the neighbourhood. Every day the bus she caught to her placement at Wythenshawe hospital would drive right through the estate. Many, many times she would feel the Holy Spirit stirring compassion in her heart for the young people growing up in those streets without love and without hope.

Dave and Colette's decision was that they would get married in mid-October and together move into Benchill, trusting that the rest of the team would gradually begin to fit together around them. Another family from the partner church backing the project, Nick and Yvonne Carrington and their two young kids Alex and Jenny, had already moved into the area about six months earlier and had built some good relationships in the community, particularly with the local housing office. Their good standing, encouragement and support was tremendously valuable, not only to Dave and Colette but to the dozens of other Eden volunteers who would follow them in the next couple of years.

During a meal at Nick and Yvonne's the week before moving in, Dave got to take an impromptu viewing of his new house. The house that the council had assigned him was next door to Nick and Yvonne and they were doing their best to keep an eye on it as empty houses were a magnet for all sorts of mischief. The sound of a commotion outside got everyone's attention. Opening the door they saw a gang of teenage lads running out of the back of the empty house and disappearing into the wildly overgrown privet hedge at the bottom of the garden. The lads had prised open the steel security shutter protecting the back door of the vacant property so it seemed like a great opportunity for Dave to take a look around his new house. It's fair to say that Dave was pretty annoyed to find that the lads had been stripping the house of its copper pipes during the raid – worth a few quid at the scrap-metal yard. But it would take more than that to stop him moving in. So what if it would be the best part of a month before the council were able to replace the boiler and fix the central heating system that the lads wrecked that night? If cold showers and extra jumpers were the price to pay for obeying God's call on his life it would be well worth it.

The Day It Rained

And where do I fit into the story? Well, because of my family roots Wythenshawe had been familiar to me from a very early age. But although the estate had been home to my grandparents and to my mum, it had never been my home. My granddad, a lifelong factory worker, saw the value of education as a means of emancipation and encouraged Mum to strive higher than the general malaise of her peers. She did, which provided her with an exit point, and as a result my childhood was very different to hers. My formative years were rural rather than urban; my sisters and I still grew up on a council estate, but a council estate on the edge of heaven, or the edge of the Peak District to be more accurate.

My own commitment to joining Eden and returning to 'live in the land of my forefathers' was sealed on a typical Manchester summer afternoon. Together with Dave and Colette, plus Nick and Yvonne and a bunch of student friends from church, we'd been spending every day running holiday activities for the local kids. My job on this particular day was to look after the 5-a-side football happening in a large steel multi-sport cage, the indestructible sort that you only find in council estates and prisons. Throughout the afternoon the clouds in the sky had been turning progressively thicker and blacker until the inevitable happened. Rain – hard, heavy rain, whipped by a ferocious wind. The next few minutes are a bit of a blur – giddy shrieks and screams, bodies running in all directions, colourful equipment hastily being thrown into the boots of cars. Strangely though, my feet seemed rooted to the spot, and before I knew it the park was empty, except for me, and two young brothers, looking at each other, getting very wet. For a moment we watched as the cars pulled away and the final few doors of the homes surrounding the park slammed shut.

Human communication is a remarkable thing. So much can be said without any words being exchanged. That was exactly what happened next. These two boys, probably aged eight or nine, fixed their eyes on me and I instantly got the message, "When are you going to leave us?"

Throughout the week I'd found out a fair bit about these two boys: the family was well known to social services as being 'at risk'. Their younger siblings were already in care. We'd had a couple of run-ins during the week with their mum's latest boyfriend – an aggressive, foul-mouthed character, frequently off his head on drink and drugs. He was the latest in a series of bad-news guys in her life. I walked the boys home, just around the corner, and with a heavy heart watched them walk up the path towards the door before turning around to begin my own walk home.

During the next half an hour a number of things happened simultaneously. Firstly, and most obviously, I got wet, utterly soaked to the bone. Yet there's something about walking in the rain that stirs the soul – it becomes a primal battle against the elements, and it's great fuel for prayer. One of the first things I ever learned about prayer came from an *Every Day with Jesus* book that someone gave me when I was a young Christian. The quote I remember went a bit like this: 'Prayer is aligning yourself with the will of God.' Well, every step I took on that wet afternoon seemed to bring me into closer alignment with what God wanted. I began to realise things that hadn't occurred to me before. I recognised for the first time that the couple of miles that I lived from the estate may as well have been a thousand miles, socially and economically. I saw that my short-term elastic forays into the estate weren't ever going to make a difference to these kids. Yet I clearly sensed that God had designs for their lives, as he did for their whole community. By the time I arrived home I knew that God was inviting me into an adventure – an opportunity to leave my home comforts behind to become part of their world. I was up for it, but how would it happen?

Imagine how I felt when I first heard Andy Hawthorne share the Eden vision just a few weeks later. This adventure I felt myself being called into didn't have to be a solo journey, and its success wouldn't depend on me. If Andy was putting his weight behind it, and bringing the full resources of The Message Trust, I could simply get involved and do my bit. To a twenty-something fresh out of uni without any real experience of urban mission, that sounded like a great deal. In the following months Dave, Colette and I, along with lots of others feeling the call of God on their lives, started meeting regularly to pray and to plan our moving into the neighbourhood. Who would our new neighbours be, what kind of reception would we receive, would the local teenagers be remotely interested in us? We'd soon find out.

How Eden became part of my world, by Princess

The first time I met anyone from Eden was when Jen and Ian moved into our street. A removal van pulled up and me, my little brother, and my mates were all watching. We were being a bit cheeky and when the van was opened we managed to get inside the back of it. There was all sorts of stuff in there, including a piano. We thought it was really funny to try to play a tune on it. They probably thought we were trying to rob stuff but we were just having a laugh.

Back in those days we used to call Jen and Ian 'moshers' because they wore baggy jeans and nobody round here wears them. That name stuck for quite a while, as well as 'trumpet-trousers' which was pretty funny too. One of Jen's friends on the Eden team had dreadlocks which was even more weird, I'd never met anyone with dreadlocks before.

I remember when I was ten, in Year 6, I had a celebration assembly because I won an award at school. I could invite someone to come but my mum wasn't up for it so I thought I'd invite Jen and Ian. They came along and supported me and Jen did this big cheer at the end, which made me feel good, but was a bit embarrassing too.

My dad was a taxi driver and worked nights so he was mostly around during the day and I saw quite a lot of him. Then he went to jail, and we used to go and visit him, on a Friday. He got moved jails though, all the way up to Preston, which made visiting harder. My mum went to see him one Friday and he complained to her of getting headaches and stuff. The following week I came home from a school trip and saw police cars parked up near our house. I wondered what was going on, I had a strange feeling that it was to do with my dad, which it was. They'd come to tell us that he'd died in prison that weekend, in fact the very next day after my mum had seen him. That was a long time ago now, ten years – it still affects me, but not as much now.

My mum coped really well looking after me and my brother, she was really brave. She also found out that my dad had been having affairs and had loads of other kids. Around this time I went off the rails, I was really angry about everything that had happened. My school life started going down the drain. I was always getting suspended and hardly ever wanted to go in. Mum started drinking quite a lot. Then she met this guy called Steve and started drinking even more. That affected my relationship with her and made me even more angry. She'd be drunk, we'd be arguing, and I would take out my anger by smashing things up in the house. One day I came home and Steve had hit my mum and dragged her down the hallway. The police were there. I thought Steve was in the back of the police van so I went up and started kicking it, but he wasn't in it. Suddenly he turned up. For some reason there was a table leg lying in the street so I picked it up and smacked him on the head with it. He punched me in the side of the face and pushed me into the fence. I hit him again and he ran off.

My mum promised me that it was over between them, but he came back again. It all started to happen again, then she'd kick him out, then he'd be back again. I absolutely hated him but I couldn't do anything about it.

The first time I decided I wanted to become a Christian was on Jen's doorstep, but I didn't do much about it at that time. It was a while later when I joined in an activity called Road Trip that things started making sense for me. We used to go on a different trip every week on an old minibus. Ian took us to a Lexus showroom and we got to see inside all the cars. We talked about how the designer designed the car and how he wanted it to look and the purpose he designed it for. It totally made sense to me. I got baptised and confirmed, they were really important moments for me. I also started going to Soul Survivor every summer which was great for building my faith.

I started having mentoring sessions with one of the other women on the Eden team. We met up every week and talked about my school and my anger and stuff like that. We used to pray about my mum and Steve all the time. I had a little God-book that I used to write notes in. All the time I was writing "God please get rid of him, get him out of the house." One day I woke up and my mum and Steve had been drunk the night before. We had one of those tellies at the time that you put money into, it had a box on the side that the coins went into. Well, the box had been ripped off and all the money had been taken. Steve had gone. He never came back.

I'm sure that Steve's leaving was because we'd prayed and prayed and prayed about it.

I don't live with my mum any more, I moved in with my uncle, and that actually means that I get on with my mum so much better. She still has a drink now and again but nothing major. She's been with a guy for three years now and he's a really nice guy. I worry about my brother, he just sits around smoking weed all day.

I'm working now, in a call centre, in Manchester, it feels good to be working and earning money. I've been saving up to go to Egypt; my passport should be arriving any day now. I've never been abroad before so it's going to be great. I'm also aiming to pass my driving test this year.

Downwardly Mobile

Dave and Colette's story, and my own, and the stories of kids like Princess, are small facets of a much larger whole. Hundreds of tales can now be told of those who have joined Eden and intentionally become downwardly mobile, adopting disadvantaged communities as their new homes. As they have followed Jesus in this way thousands of lives have been touched and transformed. The book you have in your hands gives an opportunity for some of their stories to come to light. And they need to come to light. Not for the fame or glory of those who feature in them but because of the hope they offer to everyone who yearns to live out an authentic, meaty Jesus-life, in today's world of candyfloss Christianity.

You'll discover in these pages that the people who have joined Eden teams in the last few years aren't some kind of elite Christian SAS parachuting in to Britain's equivalent of Baghdad with boot polish smeared on their cheeks. They're actually just ordinary people, reaching out to ordinary people. The only thing that's unusual really is that the places they've chosen to live aren't the places Christians usually choose to live. And the people they've chosen to share their lives with are not the people Christians usually choose to share their lives with either.

CHAPTER TWO

MULTIPLI-CATION BEGINS

By faith Abraham, when called to go to a place he would later receive as his inheritance, obeyed and went, even though he did not know where he was going. By faith he made his home in the promised land like a stranger in a foreign country.

Hebrews 11:8-9

The task of redeeming our cities will be accomplished on the ground, one block at a time, by courageous people who take the daily risks that bring life to their corner of the world.

Robert D. Lupton

Holy Opportunism

There's hardly a day that goes by when our central office doesn't receive a request from an individual or group wanting to come and see what Eden's all about. It's a full-time job keeping up with them all and so sadly we have to say no to a large proportion. I lost count a long time ago of how many people I've walked around the estates of Manchester with, and I'm sure many of my colleagues have too. One visit however was particularly memorable – I think it must've been around 2003. We'd done what we often do and doubled up guests on the same day in order to make best use of our time. On this sunny summer day my guests were Joel Edwards, then president of the Evangelical Alliance, and an enthusiastic cop from the Metropolitan Police called John Sutherland, at the time an Inspector, I think.

Our first stop was Langworthy Road in Salford, location of the second Eden team and also of the LifeCentre, a cool youth-themed café on the busy main road. Langworthy is often a place we take our visitors as within a square mile you'll find a patchwork of pretty much every type of urban regeneration all being undertaken at the same time. It's almost as if someone in a council committee room just said, "Right, well, we've got no idea how to sort this place out so we'll just try everything and see if some of it works."

Sitting down to chat over cups of nice strong Northern tea, Joel, intrigued by the way Eden was beginning to replicate around the city, immediately got straight to the point:

"Tell me Matt, what's your strategy?"

My response was tongue-in-cheek but not far from the truth. "Well, to be honest," I replied, "we're just opportunists. We wait until an opportunity comes along and when it does we seize on it and milk it for all it's worth!"

The rest of this chapter is an attempt to describe some of the opportunities we've seized upon that have led to the rapid replication of Eden around the Manchester region and beyond. And as I've already begun telling you a little bit about Salford, I might as well share the whole story.

From Outer Estate to Inner City

Salford is a city in its own right and Salfordians take great pride in this heritage. Geographically, it sits right next to Manchester's flashy city centre, on the opposite side of the river Irwell, and stretches out west from there along the northern bank of the historic ship canal. The city itself is a patchwork quilt of tight-knit communities each with very defined boundaries. This territorialism means that young people from certain areas often won't cross from one side of an invisible boundary to the other without a good reason.

Growing up in the middle of all this was the youth group of Mount Chapel church. Fired up by powerful experiences of the Holy Spirit during the years of the 'Toronto Blessing', they'd often continued their Sunday night church meetings by bravely and passionately prayer-walking through the dark, narrow streets down the hill from their building. In time they launched their own monthly youth event called 'He@t' which attracted youth groups from far and wide, to worship and intercede. At the centre of it all was a gifted young leader with a wonderfully dry sense of humour called Chris Lane. During one of the He@t meetings Chris saw a vision in his mind's eye – aeroplanes were flying over the local neighbourhood, and they were dropping curious bombs. Wherever the bomb landed an orb of light would ignite, illuminating the surrounding darkness. From a vantage point high above, Chris could see these lights having a transformational effect on the prevailing blackness. The interpretation formed very simply in his soul: "These lights are Christians moving in."

This was taking place at about the same time that the Wythenshawe Eden was beginning to gain momentum. To ensure that Eden's ministry was soaked in prayer, monthly events were being held in various locations. On the invitation of Andy Hawthorne, He@t became the resident band at these gatherings. Spending so much time together, conversations inevitably began regarding the viability of an Eden team becoming established in Salford. A young couple called Carl and Sarah Belcher from the Wythenshawe team said they'd be willing to relocate to the area to help Chris and the He@t guys get things moving. Eden number two was about to go live.

The identified community of Langworthy consisted of row after row of Victorian two-up-two-down terraced housing, separated at the rear by narrow, shady alleys. I remember the first time I went over there, it felt seriously heavy. At least in Wythenshawe we had nice wide streets with quite a few trees and the occasional park. Langworthy had nothing whatsoever that might hint at goodness or beauty at all. It was really depressing. As is typical in the inner city there was nothing for young people to do, other than wander the streets in gangs. Relief from the terminal boredom came through fighting, smashing things up, drinking and taking drugs.

Local residents had endured these issues bravely but with zero investment, empty properties had become endemic. People were desperate to get away and start afresh elsewhere but many were stuck where they were because negative equity ruled. In a full-page article *The Guardian* reported, "Not long ago, houses round here were changing hands in pubs… People were saying,

'Here are the keys – give me a couple of thousand pounds.'"
The only upside to all this was that Eden team members moving
into the area could get a property with a short-term loan rather
than a mortgage.

The move-in dates of the team coincided with this part of
Salford being named as a government regeneration zone. The
area was recognised as being in a state of acute need and so
millions of pounds were allocated to be pumped into the area.
Nobody knew at the time the scale of the changes or challenges
that regeneration would bring, or how long the process would
take. Indeed some of the promises made around that time were
still waiting to be delivered more than ten years later. Teenagers
living in the area now have been basically living on a building
site for pretty much their whole lives.

Being only the second Eden team there was a lot riding on
this initiative. No one could predict with any confidence whether
the model that was starting to have an impact in Wythenshawe
would translate to another location. Three major methods of
youth engagement were intentionally carried over: schools work,
street work and centre-based work.

From day one the team put loads of effort into the local
high schools. Do bear in mind that this was the back end of
the nineties, before innovations such as City Academies and
the 'Building Schools for the Future' programme had been
dreamed up. These were inner-city schools built in the sixties
with draughty corridors and leaky roofs, and they faced a
messy tangle of issues from chronic truancy through to serious
classroom violence. The Tribe were still doing their thing at this
time and the new Salford team made good use of them. Working
in the school was massively helpful in terms of becoming known
amongst large numbers of local teenagers and gaining insight

into their issues. One young person we met around that time was Jenny, who'll tell her story in just a minute.

The team blended this approach with a busy programme of detached street work. Walking in small groups around the eerie streets at night also proved to be a great team-building exercise! During the first year of the project the team were out four or five nights a week meeting the local youth who were hanging around. The team were making themselves visible and beginning to reclaim the streets. However it became clear that a base was needed for these young people, because the potential for really meaningful work on the street was limited. Having somewhere the young people could come to chill out, learn some skills and engage in issue-based workshops would really help.

A feasibility study was commissioned into the possibility of creating a youth centre in the area – what it might look like and what it would offer. The solution was the renovation of an empty shop-front premises situated on the main road running through the estate. The LifeCentre was officially launched during the buzz of a huge youth event called The Message 2000. The shop's interior was kitted out as a state-of-the-art youth base with a café area, video games zone, an IT suite, DJ workshop, and an arts and crafts room, plus offices for the team. In a significant first for Eden, a big chunk of the funding came from the local regeneration budget – quite a coup at the time as it was unheard of for a 'wacky faith group' to be trusted with so much cash!

Small house, big dreams, by Jenny Brown

I grew up in a small house in Salford with my mum, dad and seven siblings. Where we lived was one of those places where people never wanted to park their car. Drug and gun crimes were not uncommon. None of my family were Christians – my sister and I went to church at Christmas and Easter but that was it.

On 30th October 1999, at the age of 12, I attended a concert which followed a week where The World Wide Message Tribe had led all the RE lessons in my school. Towards the end of the evening, Deronda from the Tribe sang a song and we were all asked to listen to the words and watch a video where Christ was crucified. After the song we were asked if we wanted to become a Christian. To be honest, I didn't really understand what I was signing up for but I knew that I needed God and he would help me if I went and prayed that prayer.

Afterwards I got chatting to one of the Eden team who helped me understand what I'd done and invited me to their church the next day. So that Sunday I went along. The same lady was waiting for me, and after a little while the church became my spiritual home.

A little time after that the LifeCentre opened and I took part in all the activities: I remember 24-hour prayer sessions in the loft, as well as learning how to be a DJ and how to touch-type, but my favourite activity was always Michele Hawthorne's arts and crafts. In December 2001, after lots of love, encouragement and support, I felt ready to take the plunge and be baptised.

In the years that followed, I became a volunteer on the Eden Bus which I used to go on as a younger teenager. I also began volunteering at The Message's major events in the summer. It was great to be involved, to be useful and part of a team. Most of all though I wanted to be become a nurse, so I enrolled at college. After a lot of hard work I completed my vocational training and started full time on the wards. That was a few years ago now and my career's going really well. I now work in Manchester's biggest children's hospital where my current specialities are neurosurgery, neurology, spinal, orthopaedics and trauma.

Back To Where It All Began

Eden number two in Salford had barely begun before a further opportunity presented itself, this time in the inner Manchester district of Longsight, the very place where Andy and Simon had had their factory in the late 1980s. Like all fashion fads, boom had eventually turned to bust and with that the factory in Longsight had closed, along with that chapter of Andy and Simon's involvement there. However, an ember still burned in their hearts for the youth of this incredibly needy corner of the city, an ember that would, in God's timing, burst into flame again.

As one of Eden's principal architects, Andy was fielding lots of calls from leaders interested in what was going on in Wythenshawe and Salford. One such call came from a guy called Colin Baron who was known as one of the few pioneering church planters operating in Manchester in the late nineties. As is often the case when two visionary leaders meet it isn't long before dreams and schemes emerge. It turned out that Colin, who had planted a church that was doing quite well in the well-heeled suburb of Didsbury, was feeling stirred up about the desperate poverty just a few miles away in Longsight. The Eden model seemed to be exactly the kind of approach that ought to be used. Another piece of the jigsaw fell into place when Colin revealed that he already knew a fantastic couple, Dan and Kit Leaver, who had a passion for the neighbourhood and a flair for relational ministry amongst young people and families. It was a gift. After all, one of the biggest challenges in establishing a new Eden team is finding the right leadership. This really seemed to be green lights all the way.

One of the challenges in the implementation of this new Eden was how to get the geography just right. Longsight is a fairly big area, split into chunks by busy arterial roads in and out of Manchester. Each patch has a distinct identity, some of which were being reached by local churches, and others that clearly weren't. Positioning for maximum impact and minimum duplication was key at this stage. The discipline of spending time getting details like this right has become an important part of developing every new Eden team now. In this instance, a remnant of dingy terraced streets that had miraculously survived the 1940 Christmas blitz was chosen as the target area. A big plus for the new team was the positioning of a nearby park that would prove really useful for the development of sports programmes and community events.

One feature of the Longsight venture was that, unlike the two previous Edens, this partner church didn't have a particularly specific geographic identity – other than the 'South Manchester' referred to in its name. In time it became apparent that there were strengths and weaknesses inherent in this situation. One of the major positives was that the Eden team seemed to have a catalytic effect within the larger body of the congregation. Inspired by the sacrificial lifestyle the Eden team demonstrated, about a dozen members of the congregation also decided to intentionally move into Longsight. They didn't take on the title of Eden team members but did commit wholeheartedly to supporting, encouraging, praying, and reaching out – often to those beyond Eden's primary focus, like younger kids, families, and the elderly.

Holy Pandemonium

Deep in Eden's DNA is a sense of going to where we're most needed. Sometimes the places of need are highly visible in the landscape of the city – grotty sixties tower blocks being the classic example. Often, though, urban planners work hard to hide the poor in order to give a town or city an appearance of propriety. This was the case with Eden Swinton. The team here focused on a small pocket of deprivation known locally as 'the Valley'. A small 1930s council estate, it had one of the worst reputations in Salford for being a hive of criminal activity and drug dealing. With only about 400 houses it had problems way out of proportion to its population. The Valley estate became a big story during The Message 2000 event, which was organised with the help of Soul Survivor. Holy pandemonium broke out as 1000 young Christians descended on the estate at the request of the local police to clean up the streets, gardens and community centre. During the ten days there was miraculously no crime on the estate as the entire community got in on the action. Neighbours and families were reunited; streets at war got on peacefully together, and butch policemen cried as they saw things they could not have dreamed of!

During the event it was clear that an Eden team would be needed on the Valley immediately to continue the work that had started. However, a by-product of the improvements made through The Message 2000 was that all the empty properties on the estate were quickly assigned tenants. Nobody expected the houses that had been impossible for the council to rent to suddenly develop a waiting list! Consequently it became very hard for team members to make their homes in the community. It took about six months before the team leader was able to move onto the estate, then six more to recruit and move in another half a dozen team members. Initially life was difficult for the team because some of the local residents felt angry and disappointed by the abrupt end of the big event and a perceived failure to complete a number of jobs that had been promised at the time.

Another big problem was the fact that there was no church on the Valley estate. Every Eden team needs a community of faith they can belong to, and those being led to Christ need exactly the same. The Newfrontiers movement courageously stepped up and sent up a mature and visionary leader called Howard Kellett. Soon a brand-new congregation named 'The Hope' began meeting in a local primary school on Sundays, a living demonstration of what a thriving, worshipping community of believers looks like.

South to North

A notable trend in the recruitment of people for Eden teams, especially in the early years, was a migration from the South to the North. London and the wider South East, being the most populous part of the country in terms of committed Christians, has sent many 'missionaries' up North to join us. One place we're very grateful to is Brighton, because that's where one of Eden's early pioneers hails from. His story presents a classic example of the personal tensions and dilemmas that a call from God may induce. That call may cut right across our own agenda, it may be inconvenient in all sorts of ways, but it can't be evaded or ignored.

Since the early nineties Gary Bishop had been employed by the Salvation Army to develop the youth work from their lively Brighton Congress Hall. From this base Gary's ideas could be well resourced and the future outlook was sunny and optimistic. Understandably Gary wasn't immediately switched on by a friend's suggestion that he should take a look at a new opportunity appearing on the horizon in Manchester. Fortunately Gary was open to the mysterious ways of God and agreed to take a trip up North to talk with the leaders in the Salvation Army's Manchester HQ. The job they were offering would involve recruiting and leading a team who would commit to living as salt and light in a severely impoverished neighbourhood called Openshaw. They had a codename for the venture: Eden. Whilst it sounded like madness it was apparently working in a few other communities around the city. Who knew – maybe it could work in a neglected corner of East Manchester too?

Returning from this first-ever trip to Manchester, Gary was met at Watford Junction train station by his girlfriend Hannah. In the passenger seat of her clapped-out blue Metro he confided, "I don't care if I never go there again!"

Meanwhile, oblivious to Gary's private assessment of the situation, the senior guys responsible for making the big decisions about this new Eden offered a generous ultimatum:

"Gary, we like you a lot, we really sense that you're the person we've been looking for and we'd like to offer you the job. Could you let us know if you'll be taking it by this time next week?"

With all the grace he could muster at the time Gary resisted the temptation to slam down the phone and politely requested a bit more time to think and pray about it. "Give me a month," he said, "this is a big deal."

And so, like everyone who has ever joined Eden, and everyone who ever will, Gary began engaging God in dialogue. Something was bugging him and it was more than just the potential move.

"God, I'm supposed to have free will, yeah? So why do I feel so pressurised? What happened to my right to choose?"

And immediately the response came, forming in his mind with matter-of-fact tenor:

"You do have a choice: obedience or disobedience!"

There was still another complicating factor: Gary was in a serious relationship. They'd not been going out all that long but all the signs were good for their future. What would she make of it all? Surely it was going to end in tears. To Gary's great relief, Hannah was into the idea of paying a visit to Manchester to help in the process of decision-making. They decided to travel up North together to meet some of the guys from the existing Eden teams and ask lots of awkward questions. It was November and during the long journey north it rained incessantly. Stuck in an M6 traffic jam Gary tried to kill the boredom by making Hannah a silly offer.

"I tell you what, if the sun shines tomorrow in Openshaw, let's say yes."

Ladbrokes would've given nice long odds on that one. Funny though, isn't it, how God listens and responds, even to our sarcasm. The very next day Gary was buying Hannah an ice-cream as they enjoyed a freak afternoon of blazing Manchester sunshine together.

"I could see us making a home here," said Hannah. And right there a whole month of pressure just melted away. God was smiling on their relationship and their future, and there was nothing more to decide.

A significant feature of Eden Openshaw is that it was the location of Eden's first church plant. A dilapidated old Sally Army mission hall was still standing at a busy set of traffic lights just off the high street. Despite its age and condition it provided a really useful locus for the new project. The building formed part of an enclave of about 600 houses known as the Toxteth Street estate and reflected the prevailing texture of rotting red-brick terraces. In an act of mass solidarity this is where the team of sixteen young adults decided to make home. They were immediately faced with the depressing effects of decades of decline – the now-familiar Eden landscape of violence, crime, unemployment, youth gangs and drug abuse.

Initially they focused on team building and vision, creating a fabric of interpersonal relationships – all really important stuff for a fledgling church plant. But they were determined not to become a holy huddle, and gave a tremendous amount of intentional time to getting to know their neighbours and the local youth who hung around on the street. Gary, the newly appointed church-planter, was aware that with no established 'parent church' behind them they must get out there and see lives changed, otherwise there would be no church. This proved to be a great motivation and gave the team a tremendous sense of purpose.

Now, more than ten years later, Openshaw Community Church is alive and kicking, connecting with the community in so many ways and bursting the walls of that little mission hall every Sunday.

A Method in our Madness

After a few years of experience of trying to make disciples in the most blighted urban neighbourhoods, some patterns became noticeable. As the first few Eden teams met together to talk and pray, a basic list of dos and don'ts emerged. A steering group of switched-on pastors connected to the early projects started gathering regularly to reflect and plan. Consultants from the Shaftesbury Society were invited in to help review and offer guidance. The early teams had been extraordinarily brave but had also faced some major issues – from without and within. The hope was to help any new Eden teams have the best possible chance of success. A deliberate emphasis was placed on developing a more strategic missional methodology that involved a lot less make-it-up-as-you-go.

Eden Harpurhey launched in 2001 in partnership with Christ Church, an Anglican parish church with a long history in its community. It was to become a vibrant centre for innovation. One factor that helped the team get a great start was the sense of permission given by the local community. Respondents to a community survey initiated by Christ Church conveyed a simple and specific message: "We want the church to do more work with the youth in the neighbourhood."

Eden Harpurhey's team leader, Ian Henderson, had previously been an itinerant youth evangelist. Going deep in a single neighbourhood was a new experience for him, but one that he threw himself into wholeheartedly. Over the course of two or three years Ian began to deliberately articulate a streamed approach that offered a common framework for youth ministry to all the Eden teams. In this approach young people would not simply be invited to different groups and activities based upon common factors such as their age, gender or personal interests. Rather, very careful attention was also given to where the youth were at in their journey with God. Using methods derived from the Engel Scale, Ian trained his team to discern and respond appropriately to young people according to what point they seemed to be at on their journey. In this way different interventions could be used for those who might be very hostile towards any mention of God versus those who seemed more open, or those who were regularly asking spiritual questions.

The streaming method brought all kinds of benefits: not only did it do away with the chaos and carnage of the 'open youth club' concept, it also enabled team members to focus on what they specifically had a heart for. It also allowed greater authenticity in the relationships between the team and the local youth, greatly diminishing that awful sense of 'pushing' God to the young people. Great progress was made this way and teenagers from the area could become part of groups that scratched where they were itching. Using this method the team also grew a cluster of teenagers who made personal commitments to Christ, although they needed a lot of extra care and nourishment. That's perhaps the only drawback of this model. Because it's highly customised it requires a team large enough to facilitate it – at least a dozen volunteers, preferably more. It is however a really excellent way of doing youth ministry safely and effectively with well over a hundred young people involved every week.

Alongside this highly thought out and pre-planned strategy it's important to retain an element of spontaneity too. Jen was on Ian's team for many years, and spontaneity is something she developed her own special slant on.

The doorstep challenge, by Jen Graves

Living in the heart of the community brings all sorts of opportunities but also presents some big challenges. Creating a home that's safe from burglars but accessible to local youth who want to talk is quite a balancing act, especially when visitors could fit into both of those categories at the same time! We knew from the experience of earlier Eden teams that just opening the front door and welcoming the little cherubs inside for some fizzy pop, a Jaffa cake and a Bible study could be very problematic. Young people in the inner city often travel round in packs like laughing hyenas so if you don't want the carpet covered in cola, the sofa full of cigarette burns and half your CD collection missing, clear boundaries will need establishing; and the most important boundary is the doorstep.

To help teams work out these issues in their context Eden has developed an extensive 'Safeguarding in Action' package, for the protection of both the young people and the team members. There are expectations related to accountability, gender issues, parental consent and lots of other important stuff. Unfortunately, it's not very helpful to get out the Safeguarding policy and reference Section 9 point 3(d) when half a dozen bored adolescents are standing on your doorstep wanting something to do. One day when I was caught in exactly this dilemma I had an idea – carpet! OK, so I didn't invent carpet, but I realised how it could help me connect with the young people who were constantly knocking on my door. Rolled up and tucked away just behind the door, I kept a few feet of old carpet. If there was ever a knock when I was in the house alone, or if for whatever reason it was inappropriate to invite the visitors inside, I'd just whip out the carpet and host a tea-party on the doorstep. Being ready for the knock meant my kitchen always needed to be stocked with the necessary supplies of tea, biscuits and banana-flavoured hot chocolate. I've never seen young girls consume a packet of custard creams so quickly!

And so the hours would drift by, sitting on the carpet, by the doorstep, chatting about life and school and family, talking about God and favourite Bible stories while Roxy (my dog) would sniff around in that confused dog way when there are too many smells to cope with. Of course there were times when it was just not a good time for visitors but I would always try to be gracious. If I'd just stepped in from work, or if I was just getting ready to go out, I'd go to the door and explain. Over time I learned that one thing I could never do is ignore the young people who turned up. Otherwise the letterbox would squeak open and a shrill chorus of "Jen... we know you're in..." would begin to echo around the house.

CHAPTER THREE

BEING EXTRA ORDINARY

We were delighted to share with you not only the gospel of God but our lives as well.

1 Thessalonians 2:8

Community is not the best goal in itself – it is the by-product of shared vision, activities, practices and commitments.

Mark Scandrette

Beyond Slacktivism

Those of us who are leaders within the Eden Network have always tried to be proactive when it comes to getting out there and talking about what we're doing. That mustn't be confused with trying to persuade everyone we meet to join an Eden team – that would be totally counterproductive. Rather, with real integrity, we have to constantly have our radar up, seeking to identify and engage with those whose hearts are already being stirred by the Spirit. Some would name that stirring 'calling', others 'destiny', or 'purpose'. Whatever you call it, there's something incredibly exciting about being in a place of clarity about God's direction for your life, about having counted the cost and chosen to follow. Whether the call came like a lightning bolt or a dripping tap, its presence is a common feature of all those who join the Eden teams. The lesson here is that you can have all the talents, gifts and qualifications in the world but 'if you ain't called, you ain't chosen'.

Calling is also one of the reasons why a high bar is set across the network in terms of length of commitment. We don't accept people on the basis of giving it a go to see whether the lifestyle suits. Either you're called to this life or you aren't. In the light of that revelation, Eden's mandatory five-year commitment makes a lot more sense. The five-year commitment also honours those we are reaching out to, many of whom have experienced profound brokenness and have issues with trust and vulnerability. We wouldn't want a young person from a difficult background to develop a trusting friendship with a member of an Eden team, and then have that team member walk out of their life. That would risk leaving that young person more damaged and vulnerable than they were before we met them. Eden's recruitment process has therefore become a well-developed exercise in discernment.

In practice then, becoming an Eden team member means making a lifestyle choice – trading in a life slanted toward personal comfort, security and self-advancement for a high commitment, sacrificial, community-oriented lifestyle. Those who take this decision are immediately a massive provocation to their peers. After all, we live in what has become known as the 'slacktivist' generation. Slacktivists are sometimes also known as 'clicktivists' because the closest many young adults today ever get to actually doing something about an issue is to join a Facebook group. The point is that until we get into the proximity of the problem, until we get too close for comfort, nothing is going to change.

Achieving growth over the years has meant working hard to bust the myth that you need to be some sort of superhero to be part of Eden. Everything that Eden has ever achieved has been brought about by ordinary people who have been willing to do something 'extra' – to be extra ordinary. Nobody should say 'it's not for me' because anyone can do it, and also because 'never' is the most dangerous word you can say within earshot of God! Of course, it would be misleading to suggest that Eden is an appropriate next step for the fainthearted or the restless, as it clearly isn't. There is however a profound fulfilment found in the act of throwing away your armchair, taking up your cross, and living for something far greater than the world around you. As we'll see, Eden team members have exchanged their own ambitions and agendas for promises of "...streams in the wasteland...." These interwoven ideas then, of hearing a calling, of making a commitment, and of exchanging personal comfort for engaged community, may be why Eden has been referred to on occasion as a twenty-first century Urban Missionary movement.

Room for one more, by Simon Allison

We're quite a large family and we've lived in Arbourthorne for quite a long time now. On one level we have an identity because of the youth work we do, everyone knows us, and they know we're Christians. We're known for more than that though, we're known as parents. We're quite a colourful family, we have a lot of fun, our kids knock around with the kids on the estate. My wife Steph and I like our kids to know they can invite their mates around the house and so we have a constant stream in and out of the door, from 3- to 15-year-olds.

Our kids are natural connectors and that builds lots of bridges into different families and brings about lots of relationships. They reach all sorts of kids that we can't reach. It's dangerous though because it meant that we ended up getting even bigger as a family! On top of the four kids that we're biological parents to, we also adopted a lad from the community, a boy our son and daughter became friends with. This lad started to come round to our house a lot and as we got to know him we realised that he really wasn't being cared for. It's a sad and complicated story and for all sorts of legal reasons I can't talk about it in a book. God spoke to me and my wife independently and told us that we needed to make room in our family for him. God reminded us that he's big on adoption – after all he adopted us into his family! The bottom line is Joseph's part of our family now and we love him like our own.

Transformation from the Inside Out

Central to Eden's ethos is the belief that in our participation in the transformation of a deprived neighbourhood, the best and most lasting change always comes from the inside out. This is how change comes in an individual human life and it's how change comes to communities too. The communities we've deployed teams into have had all sorts of things done 'to' them. But never has anyone with skills and resources been willing to enter the struggle of that community by adopting it as their home. Yet, as far as the Eden teams are concerned, that's exactly what they feel called to do. During the Eden Network's first decade well over 300 people joined Eden teams and aligned their own destiny with that of a struggling inner-city neighbourhood. That number's probably getting closer to 500 now, which makes Eden one of the largest missionary-sending movements in our nation for about a hundred years.

Contrary to popular belief, the girls and guys who make up our teams aren't all gullible graduates that we kidnapped from summer conferences down South! Eden team members represent the full breadth of Britain's cities, towns and villages, their varied accents being a source of constant amusement for the local kids. Many have also joined teams from other nations of the world including parts of Europe, America, Africa and Australia. The minimum age for an Eden team member is 18, although it's really unusual for us to accept anyone that young unless they really do have an exceptional level of maturity and a quality of life experience. There's no upper age limit and so as long as an applicant can show an ability to relate to youth, grey hairs won't be a problem. Many people were inspired by Liza Fawcett, who in 2002 became Eden's first granny recruit – relocating from Chorleywood to Harpurhey at the age of 73!

Every shade of the social spectrum is represented, from self-described 'chavs' through to Oxbridge grads and even the heiress of an ancient Scottish estate (complete with stately mansion, riding stables, botanical gardens and swimming pool)! Where else but in the kingdom of God could all these people enjoy the buzz of serving shoulder to shoulder? The key element everyone shares is a stake in Eden's vision, of making a redemptive home in the heart of a difficult community. To this they are totally devoted, deliberately choosing to live a counter-cultural lifestyle in the face of some of the highest crime, drug and alcohol dependency, teen pregnancy and unemployment rates in the country. From the base of their homes they daily reach out to the youth and families of their area, giving of their time in the hope of bringing about lasting change. Deep in the psyche of every team is faith that through such efforts their neighbourhoods will see transformation as God's love thaws people's hearts.

Over the years the recruitment of team members has consistently been our biggest challenge. There was a special season of rapid growth at the end of the nineties, helped along by the favour we enjoyed at that time from friends in ministries whom God had gifted with the ability to gather large audiences. However, since we crossed the millennium, finding people for our teams has been a hard slog month after month, year after year. And let's face it, Eden's call to downward mobility flies in the face of every self-preserving instinct that our contemporary culture works so hard to inculcate from our earliest years. We're not exactly making it easy! Yet every now and then something comes along and gets me excited.

I remember a couple of years ago when Shane Claiborne's book *The Irresistible Revolution* burst onto the scene. It seemed like every Christian young adult in the country was reading it. I thought to myself, "Finally! This is it! All these folks are going to read this book and then want to move into a poor urban neighbourhood just like Shane did!" So I started watching the recruitment stats even more closely than I normally do to see if any improvement was discernible. It wasn't. So I made sure we got involved in a tour Shane was doing in the UK. He came and the events happened, and they were great. But no applications. Hugely frustrating!

Making Tents

Eden's model of ministry is to try to achieve long-term sustainability by being as lightweight organisationally as we can get away with. Every Eden team has a team leader, generally employed by the local partner church in that capacity full time. The team leader sets the vision and direction and acts as a motivator and manager toward the other team members. We've found that the work is more sustainable when we don't depend on lots of paid staff doing the work but rather harness the energy of committed volunteers. This is more than just a pragmatic way of staying afloat financially. We actually believe it to be a biblical way of operating.

In the New Testament, especially in the book of Acts, we get a glimpse of the way the early church grew and spread rapidly. Always in the thick of the action was the Apostle Paul. It's from Paul, whose practical vocation was making tents, that we get the concept of 'tentmaking missionaries'. Tentmakers are people with a trade or career that enables them to be financially secure whilst offering free time to local ministry. That's why, when we're recruiting for Eden teams, the invitation is to become more than just a volunteer in the classic sense – we're looking for tentmakers. The downside is that this model sometimes rules out younger people such as students who aren't yet earning enough to cover their share of the rent and bills.

The large majority of our Eden team members live this way, working at some profession or career in order to pay the bills, and then giving whatever surplus time they can make available to reaching young people and their families in the neighbourhood. Amongst the teams there are GPs, teachers, midwives, students, factory-workers, accountants, administrators, hotel managers, nursery nurses, checkout girls... even a guy called Paul who makes tents (yes, really!).

Living in two worlds, by Laura Jones

My 'day job' is working for the council as a Child Protection Social Worker. Yes, it's horrendously stressful! I have to really work smart to balance this with my life as part of the Eden team. It's also a challenge because a lot of the families that I work with in my professional life I also bump into on the street. That can be tricky at times. There was one especially difficult incident when I had to make a referral to the Children's Services directorate about one of my neighbours. I'd begun to recognise that the mother wasn't coping well and the kids were suffering as a result. The family clearly needed some proper help and support but would never ask for it. I felt it was important not to make the referral secretly, so I found an opportunity to speak to the mother. She sort of understood but it wasn't an easy conversation at all for either of us. It was the right thing to do though as it prevented the situation with the kids going from bad to worse.

Part of the challenge for me is how to switch off from my

work mentality – being part of an Eden team is different from being a social worker – both different means and different ends. Sometimes the boundaries aren't clear and that can be quite hard. There are great advantages when I'm connecting with people with my 'Eden hat' on though – I can be more myself – and of course I have the freedom to talk to people about God which I'm not allowed to do in my day job.

There are lots of advantages to founding a ministry on the tentmaking principle – here are a few:

It provides the team member with a daily routine and prevents the feeling of becoming overwhelmed by the demands of 'full-time ministry'.

It sends out a great signal to local youth in the neighbourhood who often have very few role models in their life who work for a living.

It affords the opportunity to build larger, more sustainable teams, as each team member isn't an additional salary to be fundraised towards.

By pooling their diversity of talents and abilities a team of tentmakers can facilitate a broad range of activities in order to affect the lives of hundreds of people in their community.

If we're going to witness the transformation of challenging urban communities up and down the country then more and more Christians are going to have to start living this way. Becoming a role model to a young person and an agent of change in a community that is struggling to overcome decades of decline is a precious thing. How amazing to think that God can take that job you do week in and week out and turn it into a means of furthering the gospel – by using it to support your ministry as a tentmaker!

Called as a Whole Family

Amongst the hundreds who have chosen the Eden path toward closer proximity with the poor, many have been families. I'm powerfully reminded of this every time we hold our annual Eden teams' away day, the time when all those involved in Eden from across the country come together. This event now requires a full-blown kids' work team to look after all the children whilst their parents engage in the worship, teaching and ministry. It's a long way from the general impression I sense many people have about the Eden Network. Yes, the larger proportion of our folks are still in their twenties but many are married and I don't know any who are sitting around dreaming of moving out to suburbia when they start a family.

This is perhaps one of the most challenging and counter-cultural aspects of the Eden call, and something I find myself frequently questioned about when out and about sharing the Eden story. Those asking the questions tend to be coming from one of two categories. The first group who ask tend to be parents of small children who are sensing a call from God on the one hand, but also have legitimate concerns about moving to a neighbourhood with higher perceived risks. The other group asking are immediately recognisable by the tone of utter horror in their voices, horror that we are asking people to 'sacrifice their children on the altar of mission!' Yes, I've actually heard that phrase used a number of times and I don't think that it's helpful language.

I've reflected long and hard on this subject over the years, along with my wife, and together with our kids. Given the pioneering role that I have within the movement we've moved around more than most and have faced these questions in different times and different places. We've also had lots of conversations about this with other families thinking about getting involved in Eden. Of course every family has its own internal dynamics but there do appear to be some common concerns:

Personal Safety – will our children get bullied, or snatched off the street by a paedophile?

The Home Environment – can we physically fit in this little terraced house with its tiny back yard?

School – can we be sure that our children won't be held back educationally in a school that draws many children from homes where learning isn't highly valued?

So how do we resolve these questions? Firstly we need to have a healthy self-awareness about where we are asking our questions from. What I mean by that is that as twenty-first century British Christians we're situated in a unique historic and social position. Christians in most parts of the world and in most ages of history haven't had to worry about these issues. They simply haven't had these choices of security, home and education available to them.

And so we need to get to the questions behind the questions: where does our sense of security or insecurity come from? Are our concerns about safety legitimate, or perhaps accentuated by fear of the unknown? Our visions of the ideal home – how many square feet do we really need? Do our kids all need their own bedrooms? How much garden is actually enough? And finally, why are we seeking access to a certain school? Is it to ensure our kids reach their full potential, or are we fighting for our kids to obtain an early advantage over their peers, or even to gain access to a certain exclusive club?

Lots to ponder on.

Lianna is a founder member of our Eden team in Gorton and she's someone who, together with her husband Steve, continues to work through this stuff on a daily basis. For her, having a new baby brought up new questions and challenges.

Crash landing, by Lianna Roast

I first felt called to Manchester when I was 17. It turned out to be quite a long journey until the time when my husband and I finally applied to join Eden, several years later in fact. Even after applying it took the best part of a year of waiting until the circumstances were right for us to move to Gorton, which is the area that's now our home and where it was our job to start Eden from scratch. The waiting turned out to be really significant, and a lot of things happened back home in Salisbury during that time. Various things made it clear that the waiting was necessary and it actually served to confirm our calling.

One of the things that happened was that I became pregnant, with what would be our first child. We were thrilled about that but it did add another whole dimension to the move. There wasn't a moment where we felt like we no longer wanted to come up North, we were still certain of that, but it did make things more challenging.

I remember the first weekend following our move to Manchester. Andy Hawthorne happened to be speaking that day in the church that our Eden team was partnered with. During his talk he spoke about Eden and how people were even coming to start brand-new teams whilst 8 months pregnant. I remember thinking to myself, "Man, that's a really stupid thing to do," then I looked down and realised that he was talking about me and my bump! Suddenly I found myself thinking, "Oh, that's what we just did, that's kind of mad."

I have to be really honest, it was one of the hardest times for us, especially the first six to twelve months. Looking back now two years later I think we'd describe it as sort of a crash landing into the community. It was our first baby so we didn't really know quite what would happen, how hard it would be. On top of the pressures of family life there was the pressure to 'make something happen' – which comes from a variety of places, but from yourself really, because you have these dreams and these visions and you want to reach out to this broken community around you. The reality is that you have to start very small and become a community yourselves.

Having Jensen actually helped us integrate better, first and foremost into the church which we were totally new to. Immediately I was able to become part of a group of other young mums that were there, they were all really supportive. I did go along to a few of the mums' groups happening in the community to get to know a few people but that wasn't easy; at the time I was just so wrapped up in how difficult things were for myself that reaching out was really hard.

Even though I found adjusting to motherhood difficult, we're settled in Gorton now, we're here for the long term, and it's a very different life to the one we were living down South. Sometimes I do think "Have I made the right decision for my son?" – especially when I go back to Salisbury and see the nice parks and nice schools down there. However, I know that following God is always the right decision and that means that Jensen and our family are in the right place.

Often in the Bible we hear about inheritance and the promised land – and that's been really significant to us.

We honestly believe that by inputting and giving into our community we are ushering in a new time of God's kingdom, a better land that Jensen will inherit.

Not Just Downwardly Mobile

A common (and perhaps well-founded) criticism of initiatives like Eden is that a major emphasis is placed on those who are the in-comers to the community. What does that say about the community – does it have nothing good to offer? Clearly that's not the case; in fact everywhere we go we're keen to discover who's who, to listen and to learn the story of the neighbourhood from those who know it best. One helpful way we've come to see our involvement in community transformation is by using a framework known as 'The 3 Rs'. This model was coined by veteran community development guru Dr John Perkins, who identifies three groups required to effect community transformation, which are:

Relocators – those with no previous connection to the neighbourhood who intentionally choose to move in and adopt it as their new home.

Remainers – those who have lived in the neighbourhood for many years and yet have been thinking about 'getting out' as soon as they are in a position to do so. Fuelled with fresh vision they choose to stay in order to be part of the transformation.

Returners – those who have a strong connection with the neighbourhood, perhaps living there as children, or perhaps their parents grew up there. They return to their roots in order to reinvest in their heritage.

It's true that numerically the largest people group within the Eden teams are the Relocators, those who have chosen to become downwardly mobile, but they aren't the only group. My own story, as hinted in earlier chapters, is that my getting involved in Eden was very much influenced by my family history and the sense of Returning to my roots. But what about the Remainers? How do they feature in Eden's story of community transformation?

The answer to that question is tremendously exciting. We're now in a situation of having more people than ever before in the Remainer category: people like Tony Grainge in Middlesbrough who was reached in his late teens by outreach workers from Youth for Christ. Tony always had the sense that God didn't want him to depart from the estate where he's grown up but rather wanted to use him to bring transformation right on his own doorstep. In 2010 we were thrilled to appoint Tony as the leader of a new Eden team in his estate. Then there's Tim Royales, an Oldham lad whose parents ran the local pub that sits on the edge of the Fitton Hill estate. Despite many scrapes in his youth, including a short spell of being homeless, Tim gave his life to Jesus in 1998. He's been part of the Eden team in Fitton Hill since 2004 and has been leading their work there since 2007. There's Simon in Sheffield who came to Christ whilst in his thirties. Together with his wife and kids he's been living on the Arbourthorne estate since the 80s. Becoming a Christian gave him a totally new vision for his life. He retrained, completing a degree in Christian Youth Ministry and now leads the Eden team that is attached to the Beacon Church on that estate.

More of Eden's leaders come from challenging backgrounds and have chosen to move sideways in order to follow God's call. There's Jahaziel, heading up Eden in Tollington, who was saved from a life on the edge of the street gangs in Croydon and moved north of the river to an estate with many of the same problems he experienced as a youth. There's Gavin, who ten years ago was an alcoholic living rough on the streets – now leading the Eden team in Bradford in partnership with Buttershaw Baptist Church. Earlier we met Lianna Roast, who together with her husband Steve leads the Eden team in Gorton, East Manchester. As a teenager she found herself kicked out of home and living alone in a dingy bedsit in Salisbury, until one day she visited the nearby Foodbank run by local Christians. Embraced by their love and compassion she became a follower of Jesus and has now become a courageous urban pioneer up North.

Transformed to bring transformation, by Gav Humphries

I think part of what makes Eden teams effective at reaching young people is the fact that lots of us can relate to the challenges and temptations they face. We've been there ourselves and we know what it feels like. I grew up in a Northern town 30 miles away from the place where I'm now leading an Eden team, so the culture really was quite similar. My story has massive overlaps with the stories of the youth I'm now reaching out to.

I hit a downward spiral from about 13 or 14. My family life wasn't great – I didn't see much of my dad and he never showed much interest in me. So I started getting into trouble. It started with occasional cannabis use but it wasn't long before I was deep into the drugs world, selling drugs to support my habit. At 16, I was kicked out of my parents' home and went from dingy flat to friends' floors to living on the streets.

I wasn't someone you could trust anymore. I had a bad reputation and no one wanted to know me. But all I wanted was a relationship with people who cared about me. I got to the point where I owed thousands of pounds to people, living in a shed, unable to eat or sleep because the drugs had made me paranoid.

Without quite knowing why, I started to yell at God. I didn't even really believe in God, but I didn't know what else to do. I gave him both barrels for three and a half hours – I just told him what I thought of him. By the end I was exhausted. I remember praying, "If you are who you say you are, get me out of this mess!"

And he did – through a random meeting with a lady who looked after me as a kid, I was put in touch with a family who offered me a place to stay – and lots of love.

At one point a group from Canada came to stay; they really seemed to have something – I didn't know what it was, but I knew I wanted it. They went off down South, to Maidstone in Kent, and I just followed them. While I was there, I gave my life to Christ. Things just clicked. As soon as I said, "Right God, I'm willing to give this a go," my whole demeanour changed. My addiction to drugs was instantly removed. I was totally transformed.

Soon after, God started speaking to me about working with young people, leading to Bible training and opportunities to work in schools and the community. When I first heard about Eden, I knew it was what God had been preparing me for. So in late 2009, my wife Maz and I moved back up North to join Eden Buttershaw, a Bradford estate in the top two percent of deprived wards in England.

God longs for every community to be impacted by his community. I wanted a father – now I've got one. Through Eden, now I'm being a father to others. Plus my wife and I have just become proud parents of a lovely baby boy, which is fantastic!

A Living Sacrifice?

In lots of ways this chapter has provided concrete examples of what the Apostle Paul seems to be driving at when in Romans 12 he urges us not to be "conformed to the pattern of this world." Rejecting the story we've been sold since the cradle – that life is about climbing the greasy pole of so-called success – is the beginning of these words being made flesh. The next step is to take action in line with our conviction. That's why Paul's direction also introduces the idea of being "a living sacrifice".

The sacrifice motif is one of the things about Eden that those engaging with it latch on to most immediately. It's true that there is a strongly sacrificial dimension to being part of an Eden team – there's a cost, many aspects of which have already been covered on the preceding pages. However, as I close this chapter I think it is important to flip that. Yes there's a loss, a letting go, but there's also a gain – in fact there are lots of gains. Whilst we're only a few chapters into this story I suspect you've already noticed that this isn't a one-sided story of giving out and giving away. Those who've become part of Eden teams are receivers too, experiencing their lives becoming enriched in numerous ways – practically, emotionally, spiritually. Rather than providing a list for you, why don't you spend a few minutes thinking about this yourself? Here's a few questions that will help you process:

What three things in your life could you carry on enjoying as normal if you chose to begin living missionally in a disadvantaged neighbourhood?

What three things in your life would you have to sacrifice if you chose to begin living missionally in a disadvantaged neighbourhood?

What three things in your life could you gain if you chose to begin living missionally in a disadvantaged neighbourhood?

CHAPTER FOUR

LEARNING CURVE

I no longer call you servants, because a servant does not know his master's business. Instead, I have called you friends, for everything that I learned from my Father I have made known to you.

John 15:15

As long as the empire can keep the pretence alive that things are all right, there will be no real grieving and no serious criticism.

Walter Brueggemann

It's all good. Right?

In the previous chapters I hope it's become apparent that even since its earliest years Eden always possessed the potential to become a 'movement'. All the vital ingredients appear to be in the mix: a clear and courageous vision, a network of highly committed people, and a tangible sense of being involved in a righteous cause. If after five years Eden wasn't achieving 'lift-off' surely it was very close to doing so? Indeed, by this point in the story you might be pretty impressed; six Eden teams in five years – pushing back the darkness in some of the nation's most difficult neighbourhoods… what a tremendous success story. It's all good. Right? Yet to give you that impression would be to do a disservice to history. The truth is, five years into Eden, it wasn't on a high. Some things had actually become quite difficult and if I'm going to tell this story with integrity then this chapter can't be edited out. In fact, this is perhaps the most important part of the book, because the struggles we went through are likely to crop up for anyone who attempts to do this stuff.

Like almost every fast-growing entrepreneurial venture, Eden faced some very tough situations – battles from without and within. Some key lessons had to be learned, often the hard way. Eden had a lot to learn about being team and sustaining transformative presence over the long term. We also had to learn that growth can make life more complicated and that making disciples would demand a lot more from us than we ever expected. Fundamentally, as teams made up in the majority of passionate but inexperienced twenty-somethings we'd need to grow up, together, into what God had ultimately intended us to become. We'd have to face up to the reality that anyone can make a big splash for a year or two, and work out how to keep our missional momentum for five or even ten years.

Hassles and Heartache

The first and most visceral challenge to the early Eden teams came in the form of crime and intimidation. Without doubt this had a lot to do with the sort of places that Eden teams were choosing to adopt as home, but it also had something to do with the timing of Eden's early years too. If you were to look at a crime graph for England in the twentieth century you'd see pretty much a flat line for the first 50 years. Then, from the mid-fifties it begins to rise, steadily at first, and then beginning to accelerate year on year until it starts to spike exponentially in the late eighties and early nineties. Eventually, thank goodness, law and order began to prevail again, but the fight to reduce crime in our communities would be a hard battle to win.

The experience of the first Eden teams, at the back end of the nineties and in the first few years of the new millennium, was that they were feeling the tail end of this era of lawlessness. There was brazen criminality, particularly amongst certain families, that was going on completely unchecked. To this day Eden teams continue to deal with some real hard-nuts – we always will – but in the early years the incidents were happening with a ferocity and a frequency that, thankfully, we seldom have to deal with anymore. In real terms this meant that team members had to ask God on many, many occasions to replenish their reservoirs of love and grace as they sought to cope with the routine vandalism of their cars, frequent incidents of verbal abuse, burglaries and break-ins, and also, but mercifully very rare, physical attacks. All this meant that cooperation with the local police wasn't just a nice idea in the spirit of partnership – it was a daily necessity for the safety and security of the ongoing mission.

The Eden teams have all learned that living in an urban community with a criminal element is something of a moral minefield. Do you ring the police every time you see someone smoking a joint, trading stolen goods or vandalising a bus shelter? What about your neighbour, who you've been getting along with really well, he seems like such a decent guy, then you find out he's one of the local weed dealers! Do you shop him or try to save him? Perhaps that's why it's in the context of mission that Jesus teaches his disciples to 'be as shrewd as snakes and as innocent as doves.' In one of the more unusual examples I've heard of, Simon Davidson found himself having to use a bit of lateral thinking as he dealt with a problem involving his car....

The missing mirrors, by Simon Davidson

When I first joined Eden I was working as a manager in the hotel industry. It had been a long shift and my wife Sandra picked me up from work in the early hours of New Year's Day. Though it was late, I still noticed that one of the wing mirrors was missing from the car. Somehow Sandra had driven into town without realising! As the night before had been New Year's Eve I put it down to a random drunk, and replaced the missing mirror a couple of days later.

The following week, the mirror on the other side also mysteriously went missing. After some searching around I found it in a hedge down the road. I was hopeful that this was just another random and unconnected incident. Again I fixed it, but less than a week later another mirror was missing. It was becoming obvious that this was intentional and targeted – I talked to my neighbours and no other cars on the street had had any problems. Throughout the month this happened a few more times. Sometimes I'd find the mirrors, sometimes I'd have to buy new ones. I quickly realised that it was cheaper to get replacements from the scrapyard instead of the dealership.

It really wound me up, and to be honest at times I wanted to find out who was doing it and have more than just words with them. I eventually realised that the godly response wasn't to go and get the person doing this, but was to pray for them, and that it shouldn't put me off being in Hattersley, but rather would remind me why I was there.

After about seven or eight weeks of frustration and getting increasingly annoyed, I realised that it was less hassle to take the mirrors off in the evening and put them back on in the mornings. At first this really used to cheese me off, but it soon just became a routine, albeit a somewhat annoying one.

During the summer time we got a group of about a dozen local 15-18 year old lads involved in a project to clear a patch of waste ground in order to create a football pitch. They loved doing it and we all got along really well. For the first time my relationship with these lads went beyond superficiality, we had some quality conversations and played loads of footy.

A couple of days later I was taking my mirrors off my car when one of the lads, Mike, stopped me and asked what I was doing. After explaining what I was doing and why, he told me that I didn't need to do it any more. He told me that it had been him, he'd been kicking my mirrors off. He apologised and I could see that he really meant it. It was great to be able to tell him that I forgave him, and from then on we were able to build a great relationship.

When the heat is on

There are plenty of issues we come across that are very black and white in terms of making a judgment call, but that doesn't necessarily make it easier to work out a response to them. One of our team members in North Manchester witnessed an attempted murder in the street one night and intervened. It wasn't long before the teenage perpetrator's gangster family were at the door of the Eden house offering a large amount of money in return for a promise of silence. He couldn't make that promise and gave a witness statement to the police. At that point the threats started and these guys weren't messing around. The decision was taken for him to be withdrawn from the project until the situation was resolved – which it quickly was, and in the most miraculous of circumstances. In a stroke of divine orchestration it turned out that one of the mission teams from The Message were scheduled to be doing a week of outreach in one of the local young offenders' institutions. Yes, you've guessed it, the lad at the centre of this incident had been remanded in custody there only days earlier. Sitting in one of the band's classroom sessions inside the prison he found himself challenged to reflect on his circumstances. The penny seemed to drop for him and he decided to use one of his precious phone calls to tell his family members to chill out and back off.

All this takes its toll emotionally and spiritually and that means the support given to the teams by the local church to which they're wedded, and more broadly from the Eden Network, needs to be timely and tangible. That hasn't always been the case and consequently some good people left the Eden teams – people who with better systems of support might have had long and fruitful ministries. It's such a shame that we couldn't have done more to help them.

Others weren't the victims of crime or harassment themselves but became caught up emotionally in the tragedies that are all too common in the sort of communities Eden teams serve. Eden teams have had to attend far too many funerals of teenagers, or their parents. A year or two into the establishing of their ministry in Langworthy the Salford team were shaken by the fatal stabbing of a girl who was beginning to get involved in their youth café. Another team had to deal with the fallout from the tragic death of a girl in their youth group who was run over by a police van on the main street that runs through the heart of their community. As you can imagine the aftermath of an event like that was incredibly difficult to deal with. It's sad but true that becoming involved in this kind of grassroots ministry amongst the vulnerable is an invitation to heartbreak. However, in the darkness of seemingly unredeemable situations we often see new rays of faith shining.

This is one of the most humbling things about being part of Eden – when those you thought you'd come to reach and to teach turn the tables on you as their own faith bursts through the darkness. Allan Cocking is one of many young people now teaching us who are supposedly 'older and wiser' what it really means to follow Jesus.

Thankful, by Allan Cocking

I've got so much to thank God for – he's amazing.

Aged 17, I was arrested for robbery, attempting to feed a drug habit that had started with cannabis but had progressed to a £160-a-week cocaine addiction. I escaped a prison sentence but I was given a community penalty and had to undergo a drugs treatment course.

Thank God, I met some guys from Eden Westwood, which is part of Firwood Church; they shared the gospel with me and helped me see how I could start over.

Straight away I knew I wanted to be a youth worker too. I loved football and learned to play the guitar so that I could be in the worship band. I knew I could be a good role model to other lads and help disciple them. I started a college degree course, going back to Oldham to help at church every weekend.

Things were going great: the football ministry was going massively well and we were seeing lots of new faces in our youth work. But things started changing for me.

Around May of 2010, I started noticing weakness in my left hand while I was playing guitar. I went to get physio for a few months but it didn't get any better. As the year went on, the symptoms actually got worse – my walking started to be affected and I was finding it impossible to play the guitar any more.

I was diagnosed with motor neurone disease, a condition that affects your nerves and causes weakness and wasting in the muscles. No one knows what causes it and there's no cure – it just gets worse and worse.

People ask me how I'm doing with it and I tell them that I'm up and down with it all the time but my faith is still strong. Every morning God's given me endurance, which I've come to realise is a main part of discipleship. I'm learning that it's OK to admit to problems and struggles and to ask for help. We all need help.

My mobility and dexterity are not what they used to be but for me, the plan has changed, not stopped. I'm going to finish my degree – I passed my first year – although I obviously now need special help writing essays and so on. I still want to do youth work and still can, on a one-to-one relational basis. I'll be doing it, just in different ways and different places.

Partnership Problems

The other main source of tension and stress was entirely different. No one expected moving into generationally deprived neighbourhoods to be easy. Conversely, the possibility of problems emerging within the partner churches wasn't initially seen as a high risk. It was very apparent by 2002 that the Eden team in Wythenshawe was experiencing quite a bit of churn. On one level this was only to be expected – after all, Eden had asked for a five-year commitment and many of the original team were approaching this milestone. Yet not all of those choosing to exit the team were doing so for positive reasons – some were leaving frustrated, disappointed or hurt. That just simply wouldn't do. And yet a much larger issue was looming on the horizon.

At the launch of Eden Wythenshawe Andy had absorbed a huge amount of flak from a small group of rather conservative church leaders who were upset that the church he chose to partner with didn't fit their definition of a bona fide denomination. A bitter irony was to emerge, as the larger church body to which the Wythenshawe congregation belonged began to exert a high degree of control over the local work. At first this meant that the team members, who came from a broad spectrum of Christian backgrounds, found themselves under an expectation to adhere to an extremely narrow doctrinal code. Even as they were struggling to adjust to the new emphases, an unforeseen and ultimately fatal blow fell upon Eden Wythenshawe. A unilateral dictum was announced by the mother church: King's Church Wythenshawe, along with a number of other satellite congregations, was to be closed. Henceforth all gatherings would happen at the main hub eight miles away in Manchester centre. The announcement was utterly devastating for the Eden team, which immediately fragmented into many pieces. Courageously, several of the core married couples, including Dave and Colette, held fast to their incarnational calling, choosing to press on without the assistance of an overarching church or organisational affiliation, and they remain faithfully serving the neighbourhood to this day.

In Salford, problems were emerging too and once again the tensions were between the Eden team living in the heart of the neighbourhood and the partner church they'd all become part of. However rather than being doctrinal or structural issues as in the Wythenshawe model, these were essentially issues to do with change management. That human nature seems to prefer the comfort of existing patterns and traditions is well understood – change more often than not will meet with resistance. To be fair to the folks at Mount Chapel, they had been experiencing an accelerated rate of change within their church culture for quite some time before Eden started. Eden simply served to ratchet the change-dial right up to levels no one had really anticipated or prepared for. The key question was whether or not the existing congregation, of around a hundred or so, could transform itself in order to accommodate the large numbers of very messy and needy people being brought into the life of the church by the Eden team.

Clearly no one wanted a repeat of the Wythenshawe saga and so the task of working out a way forward was treated with a great deal of grace and care. That doesn't mean it wasn't an awkward and confusing time for the team but it does mean that a proper solution could be found with minimum collateral damage. Friends from the Shaftesbury Society who had a bit of distance and objectivity offered helpful advice, as did the ministers involved in the other Eden partner churches. The decision was made to plant a new church, sent out from, but not bound to, Mount Chapel. Neither would the church plant be overseen by The Message. Rather, Chris Lane, returning from a spell working with Soul Survivor in Watford, was recognised as God's man to lead the plant. Together with the rest of his team he was given freedom to find relationship and oversight from whatever source they felt to be most life-giving to them. It would be a fresh start for the Eden team and they jumped at it. The new Langworthy Community Church became a wonderfully vibrant and creative expression of church. From its first gathering LCC displayed a special ability to engage people of all ages and most crucially those who had never had any prior connection with church at all. The church continues to have a tremendous ministry to the local community to this day.

Sometimes Growth Hurts

Over in Longsight good things were happening. The area that the team were located in was very multicultural and the team embraced this challenge through some really innovative missional engagement. Sadly though, the work began to falter on what might perhaps be best described as 'ecclesiological grounds'. People were coming to Christ and the team felt that the next step ought to be the formation of a local worshipping community – something akin to a church plant but still linked to the larger body of the church which met four miles away. However, there was a lot of difficulty articulating what was needed and why, which complicated and ultimately stalled the process. These days the language of 'missional community' would be drawn on in such a situation but that phrase simply hadn't been coined ten years ago. In a climate where communication wasn't at its best a number of decisions were made, decisions that were intended to ensure the long-term health and sustainability of the team. Ironically, as is sometimes the case with management decisions, the opposite seemed to happen. Local gatherings were ruled out as a possibility and Eden Longsight never really regained the missional momentum that it had in its early years.

A different kind of partnership challenge emerged in Harpurhey. The Eden team there came together quickly, largely due to the efforts of its imaginative and pioneering leader. The net result was that a large number of radical young disciples were thrust into the heart of a traditional Anglican congregation that had been steadily holding its ground for decades. Whilst there were many advantages to being grafted into a well-established church with a long history in the neighbourhood, struggles inevitably surfaced. Contentions arose over the style and content of the Sunday services. Progress was perceived to be held back by the internal decision-making structures, such as the PCC. Equally, it was hard for the long-term church members to adapt to the rapid cultural change the Eden team brought in such a short space of time. This mustn't just be written off as classic 'church politics' either. The congregation of Christ Church have always been fully behind Eden and its vision, but some of the elderly members of the congregation were genuinely afraid to attend church for a time because of the types of youngsters the Eden team attracted. These very same kids had not long before been bursting into communion services with BB guns and shooting at worshippers as they knelt at the altar!

Eden Swinton eventually became a victim of its own success. 'The Hope' church, with which its destiny was entwined, was an incredibly dynamic place to be. Alongside the local residents who had come to Christ it began to attract a wider crowd of worshippers who would commute in on a Sunday. It grew to the point that its meetings would no longer fit in the Valley estate's local primary school. At this turning point the leadership took the difficult decision to find another local venue – which turned out to be three miles away. This move was fairly painless for the majority of the congregation but for the residents of the Valley estate it proved to be tough. Rather than feeling at the centre of a church in the centre of their community, they were a small minority within a larger group of people that they had less and less in common with.

Everyone worked really hard at relationship-building – none more than the Eden team themselves. But it just wasn't the same. Now that's not to say that it could have stayed the same anyway. If there's anything of a theme in these stories, it is how incredibly difficult it is to keep up the high levels of enthusiasm and energy that exist in the pioneering phase of a new missional venture. Transitions are inevitable, gears have to be shifted. The lesson is to know this at the outset and to set expectations accordingly. We have a lot of respect for the guys and girls who taught us all this valuable lesson as they sowed their lives into the Valley from the initial revival-like origin in 2000 through to the time when the work finally drew to a close in 2008.

Success or failure? by Ruth Lancey

I should never have been at The Message 2000 festival. Truth be told, even driving to Manchester that very first time, I hadn't a clue what I was even coming to, let alone what lay before me. Yet somehow, through a series of surprising events, I found myself in Heaton Park in the hammering rain battling a tent I had no idea what to do with. Little did I know about the five days that lay before me on a small, run-down council estate in Salford.

All of us at the event were assigned to community action projects in the afternoons. My assignment was to help with a huge overhaul of a pretty grim council estate called the Valley – there were 1000 of us working on the project. During those five significant days, I witnessed hundreds of tiny miracles, and some pretty big ones too – not least that there wasn't a single reported crime during the time we were there. As I witnessed these incredible events unfolding before me, I stood, observed, and couldn't help wondering, "What's next? What happens to this place when the 1000 young Christians go home?" I felt God reply, clearly, "It will be like this again, my love will flow through these streets again, but not for just ten days... every day, 24/7."

"Excellent," I thought, relieved that my gardening skills and path-clearing efforts were not in vain. Then foolishly, before taking a moment to think through the consequences, I asked God, "But who's going to stay and make that happen?" The response came with profound simplicity: "You are." The answer made my heart sink as I instantly understood the magnitude of the task before me. I must admit, I did smile too, amused by the irony, as I was the last person in the world you would choose for that sort of task. I had many plans for my life and not a single one of them involved a forgotten corner of urban Manchester. For the next eight years those plans would have to go on hold because the Valley Estate was to become my home.

Our Eden team was small but passionate and dedicated. Over those years we lived, served, prayed, cried, declared spiritual warfare, preached in word and deed, and prayed some more. We loved as best we could. We saw team members come and go; we used up precious holiday time for community projects. We faced abuse, we faced fire, we faced exhaustion; we got robbed, we stepped out in faith, we took risks and on a few occasions even faced death – all for that 24/7 love promise – that revival promise.

And now our time has been and gone. We ended poured out, scarred and battle-weary. Our faith was shaken and questions unanswered. And for what? Could it really all have been for the sake of an unfulfilled promise? Were we wrong? Did I mishear? Did God change his mind or did we simply not work hard enough? Were the thousands of hours given by dozens of team members really all in vain?

Maybe it's just my secret optimism, or simply my desperation to find an explanation for these tiring years, but as I pondered these questions, I couldn't help wondering: maybe the 'promise' was not unfulfilled at all, but simply misunderstood. The 'promise' was of a love – God's love, that it would flow around the estate every day and impact every life it touched. In a moment of revelation a new thought appeared in my mind. Could it be possible that for every day of our eight years, during every small conversation, every act of kindness, every gift given at great personal cost, every tea we brewed, every shoulder we supplied to cry on, every compliment we paid, every activity we ran, every trip we organised, every encouragement we shared, every pound we spent, every hug we gave, every smile we made, every hour we dedicated – is it possible that the love actually did flow through us and into the lives we touched?

Could it really be that for eight years, the love of God actually did flow through that place, 24/7, impacting and changing lives forever? Did we become so preoccupied with a future fulfilment of a 'promise' that we decided what it should look like, and failed to see that it was actually being fulfilled every single day through each one of us?

So when we look back, what do we see? A hell-bound estate with a failed Eden project? Or do we see the impact of eight years of God's love working through us to change lives? The Valley may not now be gentrified with middle-class Christian clones, but it is full of young men who never did end up in prison. And mums who never did commit suicide. And teenage girls who never did get addicted to drugs. And hundreds of people who did learn that someone loves them, and dozens of young adults who now know they're not a mistake, and huge families who believe in God, understand why Jesus died and know how much he loves them.

And the soil of that estate is now full of seeds, deep-rooted seeds just lying, waiting for the divine moment in which he causes the rain to fall and the seeds planted to burst into bloom.

The Five Cornerstones

In the summer of 2003 I was reaching the culmination of a huge Christian festival I'd been seconded to, an event with an evangelist called Luis Palau. Andy Hawthorne asked to see me to chat about what I was planning to do next. He shared with me that he felt Eden needed a Director, somebody whose undivided attention could be given to ensuring its long-term health and growth. Given my history with Eden since its inception he felt I was an obvious choice. From my point of view it looked like jumping out of the frying pan and into the fire. Working on events can be incredibly stressful – pressure, deadlines, budgets, promotions – it's relentless! Why on earth would I want to dive straight into a new job that would bring a whole new set of problems to my doorstep? My thinking was to check out for a year or two, go off to Bible college, to get away from anything that might make heavy demands on me. At that time God began to remind me of why I became involved in Eden in the first place. There's something about Eden's vision that grabs me like nothing else I've ever known. It just feels like Christianity as Jesus wanted it to be lived. It was an open-ended contract, something I wasn't used to, because I like to have an exit strategy. And yet I found myself saying, "Yes, I'm in, for as long as it takes."

The task presented to me appeared to be that of 'How do we manage the miracle?' The great things happening at the grass roots were often being overshadowed by the hassles and the problems. When presented with such an intense set of challenges coming from many directions it's easy to start feeling overwhelmed. I also found that there's the distinct possibility that in the process of problem-solving, troubleshooting, granting concessions and negotiating settlements, the big picture actually loses its coherence, and ultimately may cease to make sense. It was of paramount importance that we didn't let that happen; we couldn't allow Eden to die a slow death by a thousand cuts. One of the first things I did to prevent this was to organise a 'big day in' for all the local pastors and team leaders that we had in the network at that time. I invited a Kiwi friend of mine who was a skilled facilitator to help us reflect on the things we had in common, the things that seemed most critical to Eden's success. At the end of that day we had a set of statements that we'd given the name 'Cornerstones' – five things of foundational value to each and every Eden partnership.

Here's the finished list:

Eden is always **rooted in local church**; be it an existing congregation, a church plant, a missional community, a Fresh Expression or a Restart.

Eden is always **focused on the toughest neighbourhoods**; our mandate was to go to the places where the kingdom of heaven was most profoundly absent, proven statistically by government rankings of deprivation and child poverty.

Eden always involves **making homes in the heart of the community**; our posture in mission is to minister from within a struggling community as fellow residents rather than as commuters.

Eden always has **a priority on youth**; we don't work exclusively with youth but we do sense that a particular emphasis toward them is a key part of our strategy to bring transformation.

Eden always involves **staying connected to one another** as a network; it isn't enough for us to establish teams as islands unto themselves, we need each other and we need the biggest horizon.

Attaining this new degree of clarity about our unity and identity was a huge step forward. Relationships were enhanced and fresh confidence came into the movement. The fog was lifting and we started to see development opportunities coming our way again. The first few years had been a steep learning curve for Eden, but it finally began to feel like we were fit to grow again.

CHAPTER FIVE

A NEW WAVE

Our hope is that, as your faith continues to grow, our sphere of activity among you will greatly expand....

2 Corinthians 10:15

There is church because there is mission, not vice versa. To participate in mission is to participate in the movement of god's love toward people, since god is a fountain of sending love.

David Bosch

Double Vision

There's one word above all others that I think best describes the new wave of growth Eden began to experience from around 2002/3 onwards – *partnership*. I'm not talking about partnership in the contractual, business sense though – Eden's aspiration is towards a deeper kind of relational fellowship. To get to grips with this properly we really need to switch languages for a minute, to Greek. One of the loveliest words in the New Testament has to be the word *koinonia* – it's used to convey the idea of 'partnership in the gospel'. When we talk about our partnership with local churches this is what we're always hoping for. For the sake of shorthand, you might say that we need 'chemistry' – a good fit. Probably the most important area where the fit has to be explored is in the area of vision. Over the next few pages we'll use the new wave of partnerships as examples of how a commonly shared vision can become a wellspring for a wide range of ministry.

When there's a potential new Eden team on the drawing board it's always our expectation that the church or church-planter we're talking with has a vision that's bigger than merely launching the team and reaching some local youth. We'd hope that there would be a multi-generational vision, and the presence of some other ministry specialisms that combine to make a compelling whole. By listening to a church leadership define its vision and describe its 'story so far' it's fairly easy to see whether or not there'll be a good fit. For instance if a church has a vision to develop a worship team so excellent that people will travel for hours just to get a seat on a Sunday then they probably fit in Fig.1 – that vision clearly has nothing to do with bringing transformation to a local neighbourhood. However, if a leader describes to me how their church is already sacrificially loving and serving a particular community then that sounds much more like Fig.2 and we're off to a great start.

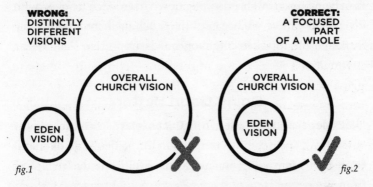

fig.1
fig.2

There is of course a third scenario, which is where the two visions overlap. This scenario is perhaps the most difficult to work out because of the temptation on each side to begin to compromise their vision under the allure of exciting possibilities. Indeed there's a fourth scenario too, which is common amongst the larger churches we've partnered with. In Fig.4 the church's vision is so expansive and multi-dimensional that if Eden were to partner with them we would just be a blip on the radar, constantly fighting for airtime amongst a host of other projects and partners, struggling to develop the relational dimension that is at the heart of our belief about what partnership is – the *koinonia*.

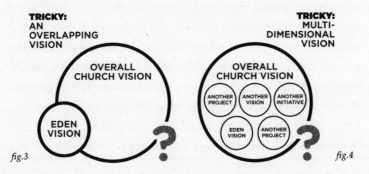

fig.3
fig.4

These models have enabled us to have more transparent and intelligent up-front conversations with potential partners, rather than being taken by surprise later down the road. Furnished with insights like these, we began pushing out again into more of the forgotten and forsaken neighbourhoods around the Manchester city region.

Doing Good Better

Hattersley sits on the eastern fringe of Greater Manchester, almost in the Peak District. It was created in the sixties as an overspill estate from Manchester, an unwelcome addition to the landscape, from the perspective of the wealthier neighbours in Mottram and Longdendale. The estate is in effect an island of council housing cut off from pretty much everything around it. The area very quickly developed a tragic reputation as the home of the infamous Moors murderers and the associated stigma has hung over the community for generations. To make a bad situation worse, many of the people in the area have lost elderly relatives at the hands of serial killer Dr Harold Shipman.

The catalyst for the discussion about planting an Eden team in Hattersley was the arrival of a new pastor at Mottram Evangelical Church: Gareth Lloyd-Jones. Gareth had felt strongly led to quit his successful career as a sales manager in the steel industry to serve God full time as a church leader. MEC was the place God had prepared for him. Here was a well-established church full of people who loved God and were ready to receive a fresh mandate for mission. Gareth was introduced to Andy Hawthorne within weeks of taking up his new post and a number of open and informal conversations about partnership followed. Coming from a business background, Gareth was intrigued by the operational model. Where would the Eden team members come from? Was it realistic to expect that a dozen or more young adults and families would want to move out to Hattersley? And did it make any sense for them to be part of the church in Mottram?

Asking questions like these led to the conclusion that this Eden ought to be a church plant – with a mixed team, some sent out from Mottram and some recruited externally by The Message. It would turn out to be a great way to launch an Eden team as it ensured real ownership from both parties, and offered something genuinely fresh and new for the residents of the estate – not another paternalistic venture from the do-gooders up the hill. Yes, these new arrivals on the estate were there to do good, but they were determined to do good better.

The Faith Works

At the time of the original 'The Message' events, back in the late eighties, a young Pentecostal leader called Paul Gibbs caught a vision for reaching out to young people in the city. In the years to come he would show an impressive ability to recruit, train and release dozens of mission teams throughout the regions' schools. His initiative, called the PAIS Project, has now become one of the nation's most popular gap year programmes attracting hundreds of young evangelists, and is even spreading internationally.

Based in the same city and with a high degree of mutual respect for one another, it was perfectly natural for Andy to accept Paul's invitation to come and have a look around a building he'd been offered as a base for the expanding ministry of PAIS early in 2001. It was a leaky old nightclub in a place called Failsworth, right on the busy A62 heading from Manchester to Oldham. It had been housing a small church congregation for several years – a church that was shrinking rather than growing.

Paul had agreed to restart the congregation and it was obvious to him, as it was to Andy, that the only future for the church was a complete reinvention of its identity and mission. The new name for the church would be 'the faithworks' and Paul's intention was that it would do what it said on the tin!

Paul took Andy on a walkabout of the local area during which Andy saw numerous similarities to the communities in which Eden was already making such a positive impact. All the symptoms of inner-city deprivation were there, the unsightly rash of graffiti, vandalism, dereliction and grime. Specifically, hidden away behind a railway line, the residents of the Dean Street estate had been all but forgotten. It was patently clear that the Hope-O-Meter for this little neighbourhood had been stuck at zero for a long, long time.

"I think this would be the ideal spot for an Eden project mate, would you be up for it?" asked Andy.

"Absolutely," replied Paul, and plans began immediately to find a leader and start building the team.

Eden Failsworth lasted for about seven years and had a great impact on many lives. In 2005 the Eden team were thrilled to be amongst the first ever recipients of an award from the Centre for Social Justice. The most dramatic changes came quite early on in the life of the project. A large teenage gang led by a hard-core local troublemaker had been terrorising the area for years. Nathan and Steve, recruited as the first Eden team members, didn't have to wait long to receive their welcome:

"Give us your car!" the ringleader bellowed at Steve.

"No," replied Steve in his thick Bolton accent, to the amusement of the other cronies in the gang.

"Give us your car now or I'm gonna stab you!" threatened the angry teenager.

"No! I'm going to the pictures, see ya!" And with a turn of the key Steve cranked the engine and coolly pulled away.

Nathan, who had the responsibility of pioneering this new Eden as its team leader, began chatting to some of his new neighbours and learned that this kind of open lawlessness had gradually become the norm. Parents were afraid to let their children play in the street. Pensioners were prisoners in their homes and nobody's property was safe. Some vulnerable residents had even been victimised in their own homes as their front doors afforded little protection.

Unknown to the gang a resistance movement was forming behind the net curtains. Nathan discovered a nucleus of local mums determined to reclaim their street. Secret meetings were already taking place with Oldham Council's new Community Safety Unit and a Christian police inspector had taken on the case as a righteous cause. Nathan sensed instinctively that great good could be achieved simply by encouraging these embattled local women to hold their course throughout the often frustrating process. It took the best part of a year to gather the full body of evidence but once it was prepared the effects were almost instantaneous. The four central characters in the gang were given ASBOs which restricted their activities massively. Any hint of foul language, threatening behaviour, even hanging out on the wrong side of the street and these lads would be serving at Her Majesty's pleasure. Within a few more weeks they were, and from that point on the 'God-colours' in that little community really had a chance to come to light.

Terms and Turf

One of the things this story reveals is an important missional principle that can be illustrated using the words 'terms' and 'turf'. *Terms* refers to the 'terms of engagement' – who makes the rules? Is it us – those taking the initiative; or them – those on the receiving end of our efforts? Who's in control? Us or them? *Turf* refers to the territory, the place in which the encounter happens – whose comfort zone is it? Is it a neutral space or is it owned? There are very few truly neutral spaces in the world so we'll probably find that the turf is either ours, or it's theirs. If we're putting on an invitational event in our church building then that is clearly our space. If we're doing a community gardening project then the turf is most certainly theirs.

Next, I need you to take good look at the diagram below:

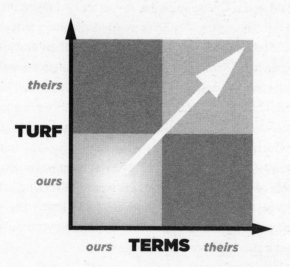

The vertical axis shows dynamics related to the turf, and the horizontal axis shows the dynamics related to terms. In each case moving out from the point of origin involves a journey.

That journey is either a journey out of our turf, or away from our terms. Or both at the same time. You're left with an obvious 'comfort zone' of our own turf and terms, in the lower left corner. When we began Eden this was our default. People sometimes talk about 'thinking out of the box', and this is certainly one box that we really do need a release of imagination to get out of. My estimate would be that around 90% of Christian mission in the UK currently happens in this comfort zone and has done for a long time.

Let's apply this model to the example of Nathan and the Dean Street mums. Nathan, as part of 'the faithworks' church, had access to the full facilities of the building. In fact, after a couple of years' hard slog, the leaks in the roof had mostly been plugged and some fresh colours inside had made the place look reasonably attractive. However, the yeast of the gospel needed to be applied in the dough of Dean Street, and not in the church's own building. It was also apparent that these wonderful ladies had started well and were feeling a sense of motivation and empowerment for the first time in a long time. Nathan didn't want to rob them of that by taking over, and yet he was smart enough to know that it could be a long road ahead and that the women would likely face tough times and setbacks. They had already set the terms for the transformation of the street – all Nathan and the rest of the team had to do was to join in with them to significantly increase their chance of success. In other words, they chose to operate on turf they didn't own according to terms they didn't invent. And here's the beauty of this approach... the net result is that the 'us' and 'them' – the 'ours' and 'theirs' – becomes dissolved in the process. Something new is created, a new shared space called 'together'.

New Arrivals, by Neil Newberry

Our first day on Pinetree Road in Limeside was the day our fourth baby was born. I was amazed how the new neighbours wanted to know who we were and why we'd chosen to live in Limeside. One of the neighbours said she hated it because of the drug houses and the abuse from other families she'd experienced. This single mum of three has since really opened up to us and invited us into her world. We helped her move house recently, just into the next street, and we believe God has big plans for her. We've also just found a venue on the estate that we can use as our church plant venue. On Sundays we now see 50-60 people coming along, including young adults from the Limeside area who have come and got their lives on track with God. Some have even been baptised.

The partnership with the Eden Bus, a mobile youth centre, has provided real credibility in the community with the young people and their families. I believe God has brought us to Limeside to have a particular emphasis on impacting children and their families. This was highlighted through our Christmas Hamper giveaway, seeing depressed families delighted at the gift. One family in particular had a father who'd been spending the family's money on drink and drugs, with the wife commenting, "I have to keep him sweet with what he needs otherwise he's violent." The father has since come to church asking for prayer, saying, "I want to change to be a better Dad," and breaking down in tears as we laid hands and prayed for him.

Signposted to Oldham

With the Openshaw Eden project maturing into a vibrant inner-city church the Salvation Army's divisional leadership were understandably excited, and wondering if the whole thing was just a fluke, or whether it could be repeated. The quality of the team in Openshaw was such that perhaps one or two could be sent out without the thing falling apart. As it happened, Chris Neilson, a founder member of the team and a guy with extensive urban mission experience, was up for a new challenge. Chris was engaged to a great youth worker called Laura from the Eden Harpurhey team and both were feeling good about starting their married life in a new place with a new vision. So far so good, but in an urban region of 2.5 million people how do you choose where to send a couple of gifted young missionaries?

In this case the answer came in the form of a financial miracle that served as a sort of flashing road sign pointing to Oldham. Andy Hawthorne was introduced to a philanthropic Jewish businessman from the town who was keen to use his wealth to support innovative youth and community projects. Never one to miss an opportunity, Andy asked him if he would provide the seed money to get a new Eden team off the ground, if it was on an Oldham estate, naturally. Our new friend agreed and so the search for the specific estate began.

In spite of its many social problems Oldham has a strong sense of identity. Its local churches have worked hard at presenting a consistent positive witness through unified prayer and outreach initiatives. Round about this time meetings were more frequent as planning was underway for a large-scale summer mission initiative called Festival:Manchester. At one of the prayer and strategy evenings a suggestion was put forward that had an uncannily kingdom naivety about it. "Why don't we all forget about what would be good for our little patch and all get behind whatever the Spirit is saying?"

A local Salvation Army officer took advantage of the pause in proceedings to explain a bit about an estate called Fitton Hill. Most of those present knew of the estate by reputation – its notoriety had even been the subject of an in-depth *Sunday Times* supplement feature that described it as a place where "the apathy is infectious." The leaders present all agreed that during the week of the festival they'd move out from their own localities to channel their resources for the good of the Fitton Hill estate. This way the week-long festival could serve as a springboard for a long-term transformation of the estate. It turned out to be a great plan although none could have predicted the truly amazing things that would happen in the years ahead, as Laura Neilson explains….

Building a healthy community, by Laura Neilson

On our estate everybody knew that the healthcare wasn't very good but they didn't really know how to do anything about it. In a more affluent area, people would write letters, have a campaign and tell the newspaper, but in Fitton Hill people just moaned and groaned and that was it. If I had just been an NHS manager looking at the estate from a purely statistics point of view, I would never have known that the problem was quite as acute as it was. However, there's something about living in an area, being part of that community and having to use the resources and facilities that the community uses that causes you to see more deeply.

We have very high levels of people on benefits for disability here – they're not working and often the reason is that there are health conditions that have never been dealt with. There's also lots of depression that hasn't been addressed, and all sorts of other conditions that a good health centre could intervene in – and yet there simply hasn't been such a centre here. Ever. So for this community access to health care was a really big deal, a major issue holding it back.

I was only part-way through my medical degree but I decided enough was enough. I put my studies to one side for a while and decided to get involved. I had a dream of a health centre on the estate that would provide really brilliant healthcare, really excellent clinical diagnosis with very high-quality doctors. All this would be linked in with good social care, church, and a sense of community, within which people could be embraced and loved. I pestered the NHS until they finally agreed to commission a health centre in the estate. But there was a twist... the NHS manager said to me that as I was so passionate to see this happen, perhaps I'd like to tender for the contract! Up to that point it hadn't even occurred to me that I might be able to do something like that, but I quickly found myself saying, "Yes, all right then, I will."

I pulled together a small team and we formed a Community Interest Company and got to work writing the bid. We found out that we would be competing for the contract against major multi-national healthcare providers. The process took about a year during which I had to work part-time as a healthcare assistant to pay for it. This was all totally new to me so I simply kept asking God to help me to write the right things. Amazingly we won the contract! In the feedback we were given from the NHS we were told that our tender included things that they 'didn't even know they wanted until they read them'.

So here we are now, running a new health centre in the heart of the estate where we have chosen to live and bring up our kids. We employ dozens of staff and have hundreds of patients. The heartbeat of our healthcare company is my ten years of experience with Eden. We're now in a position to ensure that the residents of the estate are being diagnosed correctly, and are having their issues managed properly. Kids are coming off the child protection register as parents are coming off alcohol or drugs. That's what I'm passionate about – that's what I joined Eden for!

Blessing, Belonging, Provoking

St Bride's church had a great reputation for reaching out to the community on its doorstep. With a building located at the crossing point of black, white and Asian communities, embracing cross-cultural ministry has been a necessity, not an option. Sunday services are one of the many evidences of this – full of life, colour and lots of different languages. St Bride's is a church that understands and models what it means to be incarnational. The local rector, Phil Rawlings, had been a great encouragement to The Message over the years and talk of a partnership for the benefit of Old Trafford's youth had ebbed and flowed. Another feature of this partnership was the tone of the conversation. One thing we're clear about at Eden is that we aren't subcontractors hired in to do the church's 'dirty work' for them. Here was a church that was saying, "We're having a go, we're doing our best, we're making some inroads – but come on, if we partnered it could be so much better."

Another feature of the launch of Eden Old Trafford was the intentional slow-burn timetable. Given some of the history in other partnerships we all felt that building the Eden team up over a year or two would help the new team members integrate better into church life – and would help the church culture to evolve rather than suffer the sudden shock of having a dozen new pioneers all arriving at the same time. The language was of patience and flexibility, talking up front about the issues of sustainability. It was an approach that seemed to work. Eden Old Trafford really seemed to find the sweet spot of belonging to, blessing – and also, in a healthy way, provoking – a local urban church.

"Can we borrow your cat?" by Amy Woodfield

We'd been living in our house for about two months and from day one had been building up a brilliant friendship with our next-door neighbours. They were really friendly from the first day we moved onto the estate. My husband Ben and I were in our early twenties while Donna, the mum next door, was a fair bit older, and her kids were already 15, 12 and 2. We easily got to know the whole family in various ways, shopping together, having tea at each other's houses, and having a party for Donna's birthday, as well as being invited to go and watch films and generally just be friends. However, what happened one Tuesday night solidified the friendship through an event that could never be recreated. We were sat in our house watching a bit of quality Tuesday night TV when something caught the corner of Ben's eye. To his amazement a little mouse shot across the room into a well-covered corner. After a couple of phone calls to the council's emergency repair helpline we decided to go next door to ask if we could borrow their cat! Donna wasn't sure if Buttons (the cat) was around but her eldest daughter Marice promptly brought her down from the landing. They didn't know whether or not Buttons would be happy to help out but were willing to give it a try. So with Donna, Marice and Buttons in tow we set out on a mouse hunt; within minutes we were joined by Donna's other kids, Marcus and Devonté.

For the first five minutes Donna, Ben, Marcus and Buttons searched the room to see where the mouse was hiding, whilst Marice, Devonté and I listened with much amusement to the laughter and noise that was coming from inside the room. On one occasion we heard, "There it is behind that box!" Donna's reply came: "No, Marcus, that's a plug!" Soon Marice gave in to the excitement that was coming from inside the room and decided to join the mouse hunt. I kept well away, trying to entertain Devonté and stopping him from opening the door and letting the mouse out. Ben and Marcus now had the job of taking turns to take one box each out of the suspected corner whilst Donna was stood perched on the sofa and Marice was wobbling around on a coffee table. It came to the last box and Ben was nominated to make the final move. Silence fell as Ben approached the box. No sooner had Ben's slightly sweaty hand touched the box than the mouse shot out and hid under the sofa. There was screaming, shouting, laughing and jumping around, it was bedlam!

This went on for about half an hour. We don't know what the neighbours on the other side thought was going on that night because to the outside world it probably sounded like a slightly weird and drunken version of musical chairs. Alongside the commotion Buttons spent the whole time chilling out underneath the sofa. Eventually, after the mouse had jumped from the table to the floor and tried to climb up the curtains, Buttons grabbed the mouse and, well, basically killed it. So it had finished. About 40 minutes of brilliant chaos to catch one poor little mouse. Everyone felt like they had just done a full workout and Marice claimed she'd wet herself from laughing! Once the poor rodent had been disposed of we all felt a bit bad, but at least we'd sleep that night. I don't think we ever thought having a mouse in the house could be such an amazing bridge-builder!

Quality and quantity

The new wave of Eden teams from the middle to the end of the 2000s was a great time of building critical mass around the cause. If we learned anything over those years about launching new teams, it was that no two are alike. Yes, we might have developed common frameworks and methods but every community is utterly unique. Every time a new team was added the whole network became enriched as a result. Exciting too was the feeling that we might be building toward a tipping point, that mysterious moment when change starts to accelerate with a life and energy of its own.

I find it astounding to consider that there are now more than twenty teams in the network. We're planting at least half a dozen new teams every year now, and the rate of growth continues to increase. When we began statistics were showing a profound absence of Christians in the inner city. In Manchester the figure quoted was that whilst around 75% of the population lived in the urban areas of the city, 75% of the Christian population lived in the suburbs. Eden seems to be one of the things that God is using to make sure that the salt and light is redistributed where it's most needed.

If the whole church took seriously the great commission to 'go', in its undiluted form, then every Christian would pack their bags tomorrow. The whole social, political and economic structure of the nation would be completely overturned in one fell swoop. More revolutionary readers probably read that and think, "Cool

– let's do it!" However, big numbers are not the be-all and end-all when it comes to community transformation; the right people in just the right ratios are what's needed.

Eden has always aimed to create potent clusters of people, the optimum number being around a dozen, living in quite a small area – just a few intersecting streets. It's evident that God looks after the big picture of bringing together the individual personalities and histories that give each team its unique character. And because every person who applies to join Eden is different we mustn't fall into the trap of screening according to some preconceived idea of charisma or coolness; we select on calling and character, everything else is peripheral.

What might those essential character qualities look like?

- At the core of every team is a passion to see broken hearts healed and lives restored through Jesus.
- Therefore we need a profound personal sense of the depth of God's divine grace.
- No team member arrives as a finished product, with all the answers, and there are many lessons to be learned in the community. Therefore we need a sincere desire to continually grow in God.
- Eden requires a willingness to be stretched, challenged, and to try new things, and an openness to be accountable to our leaders and team mates.
- A sense of perspective that places a personal contribution to the local community within the vision of the local host church and the broader horizon of God's big plan for the city.
- Finally, an openness to expect the unexpected and take each day as it comes.

Let's close this chapter by looking at this last point a little more closely. Undoubtedly one of the things that attracts people to become part of Eden is the sense of adventure. There's an unpredictability about becoming involved in an urban community that gives every day an 'edge'. Anything could happen, and frequently does. Of course this can be inconvenient and frustrating, and yet at the same time it can be incredibly rewarding and exhilarating. Being available to others and becoming caught up in the drama of their lives requires a special kind of openness and a certain posture toward the unexpected. On the next pages are just a couple of short examples.

I didn't expect... by Sam Ward

I didn't expect to be told by the police to wait inside the house whilst the bomb squad defused a World War II bomb that had been discovered buried outside a house on our street.

I didn't expect to have to crawl into the house of a local family I'd been reaching out to, through the hole the police made whilst kicking the door in to try and find drugs.

I didn't expect to meet a heroin addict who I later found out had been a world kickboxing champ.

I didn't expect to get invited to the 18th birthday party of a neighbour who was moonlighting as a sex chatline operator. I certainly didn't expect to be sat there with my wife as a male stripper turned up and proceeded to go 'the full Monty' whilst we were trying to be incarnational!

The Christmas Eve Visitor, by Tony Grainge

Our first winter as an Eden team was the coldest for a long time and snow and ice seemed to be constantly on the ground. This meant my windows were being pelted with snowballs regularly and sometimes as I'd try to drive my car the kids would throw snow at the windscreen so I couldn't see, or would push the car from side to side as the ice on the road was so slippery! This was also mixed with the very same kids helping me push the very same car out of the deep snow it became stuck in, and attempting to clean the snow and ice off the local paths together.

On Christmas Eve at 11:30pm while I was having a last-minute gift-wrapping session with my wife-to-be, there was a knock at the door. A man in his late twenties was stood there, swaying, obviously drunk. He said, "I need to talk to you... what is this God stuff?" So we invited him and he proceeded to really open up to us in that way that blokes who've had a few bevvies tend to.

"I've seen how you are with the kids and other people on the estate," he said, "and it's stood out to me. Why do you behave like that?"

It was a perfect moment for me to share my testimony. I'd grown up on the estate myself and had been a bit of a bad lad. I've always been into boxing and so people knew I wasn't a soft touch. That made people even more surprised when I became a Christian. But learning to follow Jesus wasn't easy and now years later I think everyone's realised that there's no way I'll be going back to my old ways.

The guy stayed for about half an hour and asked loads of great questions about God. That late-night conversation really seemed to move him on with God and we still have contact now. The only downside of the story is that when I went to the loo after he'd gone I discovered that he'd peed all over the toilet seat!

CHAPTER SIX

THE
PROXIMITY
PRINCIPLE

...be sure of this: the kingdom of God has come near.

Luke 10: 11

Mission is revealing to others their fundamental beauty, value and importance in the universe, their capacity to love, to grow and to do beautiful things and to meet God.... Mission is transmitting to people a new inner freedom and hope; it is unlocking the doors of their being so that new energies can flow; it is taking away from their shoulders the terrible yoke of fear and guilt.

Jean Vanier

Network and Neighbourhood

The great Bible teacher John Stott was fond of the phrase 'double listening'. Well, Eden has to practice its own form of double listening as it constantly evolves in our ever-changing world. The first listening is to our own neighbourhoods, and I've said a lot about that already. The second listening is a listening to what God is doing in the church more broadly. If we want to avoid stagnation we must allow ourselves to be shaped by voices from without as well as voices from within. Much of the material in this chapter has originated through listening in this way.

You may be aware that a few years ago the Anglican Church released a report called 'Mission-Shaped Church'. One of the ideas that has developed since its release, particularly from the mind of Bishop Graham Cray, is the idea of 'the new local'. In other words what one person means by 'local' these days is very different to what another means when they use the very same word. The phrase 'local church' is a perfect case in point. To some this would mean a Christian community with roots in a very tightly bounded geography. Others would apply the same phrase to refer to a body of believers drawn from a wide catchment area who gather in a place that could be half an hour's drive from where they actually live. Answering the vital question 'What is local in the twenty-first century?', Bishop Graham affirms both of these situations, saying that local has become two things: *neighbourhood*, and *network*. I find this distinction really helpful and my hunch is you probably will too. Let me explain.

Firstly let's take the idea of neighbourhood. This is our domestic location, where the basic stuff of life happens such as washing, sleeping, watching TV. To all intents and purposes, it's home, although it may or may not feel like it in the emotional sense – which is an issue for another day. Secondly, the idea of network. This would be our social and/or vocational location; the places our work takes us, or the places where we meet and make friends. These days this could even be a virtual location, somewhere in cyberspace such as Facebook! The thing to understand about neighbourhood and network is that they coexist to greater or lesser degrees in all our lives. And, in fact, the degree to which network or neighbourhood are significant to us will change over time. This has huge implications for the way we engage in mission.

Take for example one of my wife's friends, Dorota. She's young, Polish, multilingual, business-savvy and highly mobile. We met her while she was part of our church in Manchester. She's currently in Australia and who knows where she'll end up next? Contrast her life with that of Danny who I know from our numerous run-ins at the youth club on the Valley estate. Danny's a school dropout, a sofa-surfer, his ankle fitted with an electronic tag the last time I saw him. The magistrate has laid out clear restrictions on where he can and can't go, at what times of day. He's literally stuck on the Valley estate. Dorota is the epitome of a network lifestyle, and Danny a classic example of neighbourhood. A church that is full of well-educated, well-connected, well-travelled people will feel like a perfectly natural environment for Dorota – but will be incredibly strange and uncomfortable for Danny. Equally, a church made up of people who have strong ties to a specific place, who place a high value on participation in goings-on in their immediate vicinity is going to tap into Danny's need for family and belonging, but may well leave Dorota feeling quite out of place.

Arguments have dragged on for years now about whether churches ought to be *attractional* or *incarnational*, but I think we need to grow up and move on. Those words aren't helpful anymore. These short pen-portraits serve to show that today's cities need a mixed economy of both network and neighbourhood churches in order for everyone to be effectively reached. The so-called 'attractional' churches are really network churches, best suited to reach network people; 'incarnational' churches are neighbourhood churches, and are best suited to reach neighbourhood people.

Eden then, is a neighbourhood initiative, plain and simple. It works best with churches that operate on this basis. Of course, those of us who choose to be part of Eden can't immediately divorce ourselves from the other spheres of life in which we operate, but we choose to prioritise the local. We have to be intentional about this because it's one thing to move into a neighbourhood and get the postcode but that doesn't make us part of the community. There's a bit of theology embedded here actually because, in part, the way we express what it means to be incarnational is by accepting a degree of self-limitation. We may not have a great deal of control over the hours we work but we may choose to limit the number of weekends we travel away from the neighbourhood – in order to invest ourselves locally. We may choose not to travel to the out-of-town supermarket once a week but to support shops closer to home, getting to know the staff and other customers there as we become 'regulars'. The same goes for leisure time – urban pubs are closing far quicker than urban churches, five a week at the last count I think. These longstanding places of community-building can become an excellent 'third place' for us and a great venue in which to meet those Jesus called the 'person of peace', which we'll talk about more later.

The Proximity Principle

I love '*The Far Side*' cartoons by Gary Larson – it's one of the many signs that I'm hopelessly stuck in the nineties. One of my favourites shows a village of straw huts and a crowd of scantily clad natives all staring anxiously as another villager writhes on the floor. The caption reads: "Crossing the village Mowaka is overpowered by army ants. Later, bystanders were quoted as saying they were horrified but didn't want to get involved."

Larson's humour works because he takes really well-observed social ideas that resonate with us, and then stretches them to absurdity. In this example he's lampooning the social phenomenon known as 'Bystander Apathy'. Anyone who lives in a big city is likely to be familiar with that feeling of witnessing an unpleasant situation unfolding and desperately hoping that someone else will deal with it, someone closer, someone who isn't in such a rush, someone better equipped than you, anyone but you! And so nobody helps at all. The strange thing about the bystander effect is that it is an inverse law – the more people who are around, the less likely it is that there will be any intervention. If you're in the park walking by the duck pond and see a child drowning, the likelihood is that if you look around and see nobody else there you'll try to do something about it yourself. But if there are a dozen of you, each one of you will be hoping that another will intervene.

Let me just stretch this point a tiny bit more, and then describe how it applies to urban mission. Firstly we need to understand the idea of proximity – closeness. There are two kinds of closeness. There's straightforward *physical* distance – the first one who does wade into the duck pond to save the child is likely to be the closest. Then there's *relational* distance – nobody would hesitate to jump in if it were their own son or daughter or sister or brother in the pond! In missional terms, physical proximity is a good thing – being someone's next-door neighbour is a great platform from which to grow a bond of empathy and respect. But relational proximity is great too – after all, you don't need to live on someone's street to have a significant role in their life. Here's the thing: when the two intersect, the potential for transformation increases exponentially. It's about getting too close for comfort. Because as Christians we're just as prone to bystander apathy as anyone else – I know I am. We must make deliberate choices to become close to those who are living without hope and without God in this life, close in both meanings of the word. If we don't then our consciences will never become properly engaged and we'll remain in a state of apathy.

One of the best examples I ever saw of this was on a short TV series that was shown on ITV a few years ago. Four celebrities, including a film star, an ex-Spice Girl and a famous rugby player had to spend a week living with a family in an inner-city estate. The fourth celeb was Trinny – the fashionista from that awful makeover show. Anyway in her closing reflections she said something that is actually really profound. I wish more Christians would live like this:

"I'm very good at being practical and I'm very good at thinking of solutions and for me, this journey wasn't about that, because that's kind of easy for me to do. This was far more about getting to know somebody enough, to care about them enough, to want to change their life. And that's what happened."

Just like everyone who joins an Eden team, Trinny and her celeb friends all found that moving into the community is a steep learning curve. One thing that always comes as a bit of a shock in that learning process is that a lot of what we go through is better described as 'unlearning'. Very quickly we find out just how much we are creatures of habit – and the extent to which we are also 'highly programmed' as people. Like it or not we have all been culturally conditioned to think and act in certain ways. That's why the Bible is so clear about the need for 'renewing of the mind.'

One of the most apparent unlearnings that needs to happen is to do with the way we naturally defend our lives. The 'Englishman's home is his castle', after all! We can be extremely effective at walling ourselves in, creating layers of relational insulation. The proximity principle applies a constant and healthy friction that, like a pumice stone on the sole of a hiker's foot, restores sensitivity and feeling. Yet, even for our veteran team members, there's always the temptation to gradually 'pull the shutters down' over time. That's why we need to be in teams, supporting one another and holding one another accountable to the way of life that we've agreed together to flesh out.

Love Thy Neighbour, by Chris Neilson

I arrived back from work one day and straight away noticed things weren't right. For starters, my TV and video were missing. The penny dropped. I felt really sick and angry. I'd never been burgled – it's one of those things you know could happen, but it kind of leaves you speechless when it does.

The back window had been smashed and the back door was open. Amazingly I saw a police car driving by and frantically flagged it down. It stopped and I spewed some frantic nonsense at the officers. They seemed to get the picture and came inside where I spoke to them in a slightly more logical manner. They said they should go and look at the broken window, so I said I would go next door and see if the bloke there had seen anything. Immediately I noticed his door was open. I'd heard that sometimes burglars break into a few houses in a row and rob them all at once, so as a brave neighbour I thought I'd investigate.

I shouted "Hello..." but got nothing, which reinforced my belief that he'd been burgled too. I kept shouting as I walked through the door into the lounge – no one was home. I thought I should try the back room and shouted "Hello" up the stairs as I went. When I looked in the back room there was all my stuff – my TV, my video, my microwave, my CDs, my coat! The only things unaccounted for were my old Sega game system and some chopsticks I'd bought on a visit to China a few years earlier.

I shot back to my house and said breathlessly, "It's next door. My stuff is next door." The police weren't particularly surprised to hear this.

The next few days I spent a lot of time praying. When the police came back round and asked if I wanted to prosecute, I said that I did. Although I believe in a God of forgiveness I also believe in a God of justice. On a deeper level God was helping me to forgive. I was determined that after all this I was going to be this guy's friend.

Paul didn't come back for a week, obviously lying low somewhere. It was the next Friday afternoon when I came back from work that I saw him, in his garden digging the weeds. He was a rather sickly-looking guy with very yellow skin – this can happen with severe drug addiction. I spoke to him over the fence.

"Hi Paul, how are you doing?"

"Oh, fine," he said. "Just digging the garden while the weather is nice."

Let's get this over with, I thought. "Look, I got broken into last week, did you know?"

"Ooh yeah, I heard about that – terrible, in't it," he answered.

A little confused and not wanting to let him off the hook, I pushed again.

"And we found all the stuff in your house, Paul."

"Ooh, yer," he said. "Heard about that... terrible, in't it."

And that, it seemed, was a reasonable answer to the bloke you had just burgled and was trying to get you arrested for it. I took a big gulp and said,

"Look Paul, you know that I'm a Christian and I go to that church down the road. Well because of that I believe in forgiveness and because of that there is not going to be any retaliation and I'm prepared to forgive whoever was involved."

He denied any involvement or any knowledge. I suddenly remembered my chopsticks, so asked Paul if he'd seen them. "Ooh yes," he said. "They're on top of the telly." And he went back inside, brought out my chopsticks and handed them back with a neighbourly smile over the garden fence.

A week later I came back from work to find Paul in my garden. He'd spent the whole day tidying it for me. He'd also taken a few cuttings from his garden and planted them in mine. It looked great. He advised me on what I could do with it and told me that he liked gardening and if it was OK with me he would do it for me each week. He kept to his word and we had the best looking gardens in the street. Paul and I became good friends. We'd chat about what had been going on in the street and what he was thinking of doing with the garden. He didn't have a phone so would occasionally knock on and borrow mine, but he never took advantage. We'd do all the other neighbourly things like borrowing a bit of milk and sugar. Ironically he would keep an eye on the house for me if I went away.

The police took a long time to get round to anything and couldn't get any fingerprints. As we could not place Paul at the scene, we could not prosecute. If it had gone to court there would have been a reasonable doubt so the case was dropped.

Paul had health problems that meant that he was on dialysis each week. I went to spend some time with him in hospital and he told me his story. He'd been born with a kidney problem but contained it. As a youngster he got into trouble and also got into recreational drugs. For five years he was living with his girlfriend and they were thinking about getting married. Then within a year both his parents died and his girlfriend left him. With no community or support around him he ended up back with his mates. He was really lonely and depressed. At this point he got more heavily into drugs which aggravated his kidney problem and then infected his liver. The hospital gave him a transplant, which made him better for a while, but as his lifestyle didn't change the new kidney failed.

Paul's life was a mess and he knew it but he didn't have the maturity or confidence to get himself out, and his so-called friends pulled him down again and again. He fell seriously ill again and went back into hospital, but was refused a second transplant because the doctors felt it would be wasted. During his time in hospital I went to visit him every week. The nurse told me I was one of his only visitors. The prognosis for Paul wasn't good and because I knew that I didn't have long with him I talked often about my faith. He had some good questions. Paul admitted to me that he'd been involved in the burglary and we prayed a prayer of forgiveness.

Paul knew God lived in my life and he would talk about how he wanted God to change him. He prayed with me once and I really hope that he gave his heart to Jesus.

Paul was in and out of hospital for a year or so, until he finally passed away. His story reveals just how broken our world is, full of injustice, fear, despair and unfairness. I know God loved Paul and I know Paul knew that. I used to tell him often enough. I just hope that I will meet him again in heaven and we can sing together, praising God whose grace is sufficient for both of us.

Small Worlds, Short Horizons

There's something quite special about the way many inner-city neighbourhoods are constructed, which I imagine is probably the same the world over. It's not to be found in the bricks and mortar but in the social ties, and particularly the family connections. Whilst British commuter belts have developed a reputation for being socially retarded, where 'good fences make good neighbours', the estates we spend our time in are quite the opposite. In this way young people on our urban housing estates live within a social framework that's more village than metropolis. Yes, there are all the trappings of the information age, Sky+, broadband, space-age shoes from the planet Nike. But did you ever watch Star Trek? Kirk and Spock would often turn up in a distant galaxy and find a world inhabited by people who live in straw huts but have somehow developed laser beams. Urban ministry's a bit like that, a strange coexistence of the past and the future.

When they feel relationships with young people and parents are up to it, and when finances will stretch to it, Eden teams will take young people from the neighbourhood out on day trips or residentials. It's at times like these that the disadvantage of many young people's lives becomes apparent. Tragically, in twenty-first century England we can take a group of our urban teenagers into the countryside and half of the minibus will freak out upon sighting a real live cow for the first time! That's not just a measure of material poverty – it shows just how trapped and confined these young people have been for their whole lives. The net effect of this is a squeezing and narrowing of their lives in both of the principal dimensions that we have available to us as human beings – space and time.

Few people besides Hawking-type boffins really understand how space and time work, but that's not important here; spend time living inside the labyrinth of the estate and you'll see a severe limitation of both. In terms of space, many young people we get to know in the estates occupy extremely small worlds. Sure, within these worlds, defined by just a few streets and landmarks, they may display an attitude of invincibility, but outside them they feel extremely insecure. This goes some way to explaining why 'space invaders' like the Eden teams can sometimes have a tough time gaining acceptance when they first move in. In the dimension of time the same young people are likely to be equally restricted. Evidence of short horizons is all around. Living for the moment is the order of the day and future aspiration is rare. The ideas of cause and effect and of consequence may be utterly foreign. Very little framework exists for extra-terrestrial stuff like empathy, responsibility or guilt.

Imagine, then, what an amazing thing it is when a young person comes to Jesus and all that changes! Instead of the world being defined by the end of the street it begins to swell out in all directions as the awareness suddenly dawns that there is a whole global family out there offering an open-arms welcome. Instead of the horizon being limited to how long it will be before I can score another bag of weed, the impact of a 2000-year-old story flicks the switch of an eternal destiny, lighting up a whole new life-scape.

Into this context Jesus-style ministry from the pages of the gospels finds immediate application. Take the example of Jesus sending out the seventy-two in Luke chapter 10. After offering some reverse-motivational psychology, "I am sending you out like lambs among wolves", he quite deliberately introduces a local character described as a 'person of peace'. In the towns and villages that the first disciples were being sent to this was someone who would open their home to feed and shelter them. We've found that example carries over into the contexts we're working in very well. The first time you have the opportunity to step into the home of one of your new neighbours is a really special moment; our experience has proved this time and time again.

We invariably find that God has been working by his Spirit preparing the heart of a key local resident long before we ever arrived. It's important to be prayerful and discerning about who this might be. For lots of teams this person has been a teenager. For some teams the person of peace has been a matriarchal figure, with influence in the community by virtue of her large family that has branches here, there and everywhere. Other teams have found favour with a local councillor or police officer, or even the owner of the local pub or pharmacy. Quite a lot of teaching content has been developed by various ministries over the years on how to recognise a person of peace and what to do when you find them but we've never really been that prescriptive about it. All we do know is that people of peace come in all shapes and sizes so team members always need to be alert. Gaining trust, goodwill and acceptance in a community will come more smoothly and quickly if we can connect early on with one of these special people.

Family of peace, by Susie McGibbon

It was one of the first youth drop-ins and we were all raring to go, expecting God to do stuff but not sure what would come up. As we were still only just getting to know many of the young people we set aside a two-minute slot at the end of the night to share a bit about ourselves, to let them know we were Christians and to talk a little bit about Jesus.

At the end a teenage lad approached my husband Rob and said quite matter-of-factly, "Do you know anything about ghosts?" There was a bit of a hush as the rest of the team all turned their ears to hear Rob's response, "Not a lot, but I know God is bigger than ghosts." The lad went on to explain that he and his friends had been freaked out that week by the ghost in his house, and that his mum hasn't slept for years because of it. Rob offered to come over to the house with me, to pray with this lad and his mum. I remember having a complete mix of emotions such as, "Gee thanks, Rob, for volunteering me," and "Come on God, you'd better do something here or we'll look really stupid," and also "I hope his mum lets us through the front door!"

We went to the house immediately, with a few of the other teenage lads trailing behind at a short distance, curious as to what was going to happen! His mum answered the door saying, "What's he done?" We explained that her son wasn't in trouble. She was moved to tears when we explained why we'd come, and she invited us in. Her son and a few of his mates came in too as spectators.

Inside she talked about how she was scared, exhausted and desperate but didn't think anyone would ever believe her. She was overwhelmed that we believed her and wanted to pray with her. We didn't do any freaky praying and casting out, we just prayed gently that Jesus would reign and that his Spirit would live in the house. She was so grateful, and amazingly even the teenage lads sat and prayed along with us!

Later in the week we asked her how she was doing. She told us that she'd slept well every night and felt really peaceful! Since that time God has been working in a special way in that family. They have become what you might call a 'family of peace' for us and through them we've got to know lots of other people.

Love Triangles

The highest privilege that an Eden team member has is to serve their church in its mission of disciple-making. In the early years of Eden this was generally understood as the cultivation of a popular process known as *'belong, believe, behave'*. One of the reasons for the popularity of this approach was that it was seen by many to be a reversal of the way the church had sought to reach young people in prior eras. I recall reading articles in youth work magazines poking fun at churches that first expected young people to sit still and be quiet in church services, so that whilst they're sitting quietly they might hear something profound and come to believe. Finally having passed a test that all their beliefs are now in order, they might be allowed to belong. Well, whichever way you work the process, over time, Eden teams began to realise that it isn't a process at all. That doesn't mean that the '3 Bs' aren't important – they're really important – but they form a triangle and not a straight line. Let me explain…

Typically when we meet a young person on an estate they're living in a very small triangle – that is, they have very little sense of belonging to anything or anyone; they believe very little – in fact they tend to be consumed by suspicion and mistrust – and their behaviour is both self-destructive and causing pain to those around them. Eden's task is to lovingly, imaginatively and consistently offer opportunities to those we are drawn into relationship with – opportunities to grow their triangle! This is the work of disciple-making, and there are no shortcuts to success. The investment of time is counted in years rather than weeks or months. That's why living in close proximity to them and being part of their world, perhaps even on a daily basis, is crucial.

Is all this investment of time and energy worth it? Absolutely. Because as the years progress we do see our teenagers growing in all three dimensions. They develop a strong sense of belonging to a community that is bigger than they are – the church, the family of God. Within this community their adolescent identity issues can be worked out in a really natural way as they contribute to, as well as receive from, those around them. They also grow a vibrant belief in a loving God who has a plan for their life and never gives up. Over and over again I've found myself truly amazed at how quickly transformation can come to a young person's life when they start depending on God rather than falling on their destructive habits and coping mechanisms. And their behaviour, whilst still from time to time contradictory, is infinitely more healthy, a profound change evident for all to see.

There's no better testimony than that of a tearaway teenager who goes from being part of the problem to being part of the solution.

It sounds attractive doesn't it – we want more of that, please. And there's the challenge. We'll only see more young people being discipled in this way if we see more disciple-makers released into our communities. Oh, absolutely we do our best to work smart, to double up where we can and to use peer mentoring and group work too. That doesn't change the fact that there's a huge deficit of mature Christians living in the neighbourhoods that most need to feel the impact of their life and light.

How do you feel about this idea of proximity? Could you make it your goal to get closer? God doesn't want us to distance ourselves from people. How close are you willing to get – too close for comfort? Is there a certain 'respectable distance' between yourself and those you feel called to? Can you close that gap? Could you go further and deeper in the way you give, the way you serve and the way you love?

Changing my ways, by Anth Brown

I've always loved football, and during my teens I was getting on really well having been taken on to the Middlesbrough FC youth team. Things were going well and I was getting picked for the squad most weeks. Problem was I used to go out drinking and stuff as well, a lot. I had the wrong attitude about everything. The club weren't happy and released me, they sent me to Darlington so that my attitude could improve, but it didn't.

I kept on going out with my mates loads, to house parties and stuff like that, just getting in with the wrong crowd really. I was losing my way, I'd turn up at training but not be focused on the football, I was more focused on going out at the weekend.

School was a nightmare too. In total I got suspended 48 times, mainly for fighting and being a rebel. I used to do stupid things when I got together with my friends. There was this one time we were at the Riverside Stadium watching the Boro' playing a match, well a few of my mates dared me to streak across the pitch... and being the clown of the group I would never turn down a dare. The next thing I knew I was getting arrested and banned from the ground.

Getting suspended all those times did actually put me on a bit of a learning curve. The big change began when I met a guy called Tony at my mate's 18th birthday party. He asked me if I wanted to go to an event to hear an ex-prisoner tell his life story. He also said there would be free food which convinced me it was worth a try. When I heard the guy talk it convinced me that God is real and I became a Christian. Suddenly I could tell the difference between right and wrong and I matured a lot very quickly.

Now I like to help the younger lads on the estate, I don't want to see them go down the same path that I went down. My Eden leader Tony has invested in me and now I'm following in his footsteps, and in Jesus' footsteps as well.

CHAPTER SEVEN

TRANS-FORMATION

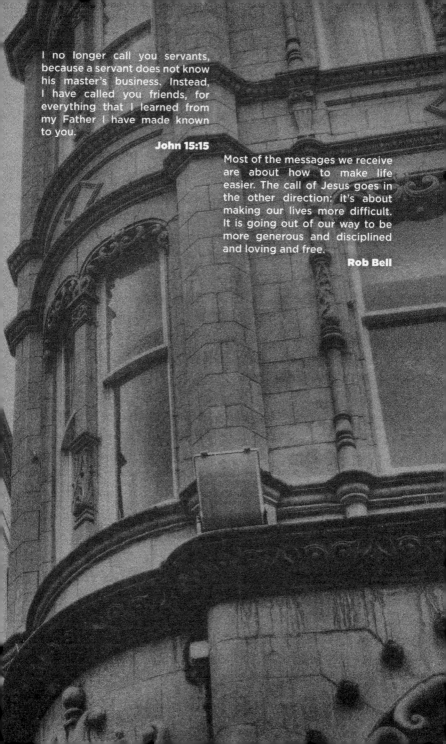

I no longer call you servants, because a servant does not know his master's business. Instead, I have called you friends, for everything that I learned from my Father I have made known to you.

John 15:15

Most of the messages we receive are about how to make life easier. The call of Jesus goes in the other direction: it's about making our lives more difficult. It is going out of our way to be more generous and disciplined and loving and free.

Rob Bell

Two Thousand Years In The Making

Have you ever read through the book of Acts? What a roller-coaster ride! It gives the impression that being part of the early church was just one miracle after another. I recall being quite disappointed when I first found out that the events it contains cover a span of about 30 years. Similarly, if you were to add together the total number of years that Eden team members have been living in deprived communities, you'd discover that Eden's been 2000 years in the making! This is the challenge for anyone who comes to 'have a look round Eden'. What exactly are people going to see by visiting one of our Eden team locations? A visit, even if it stretches over a weekend, can only provide a tiny glimpse into what's going on. Imagine just looking at a single still frame from a time-lapse photography series; the wonder of that flower opening, those seasons transforming, or that constellation working its way across the night sky would be impossible to see. I don't want to discourage people from visiting our teams – yes, visits have limitations, but guided properly they can still be valuable. No, I make this point because, particularly in book form, it's easy to lose a sense of perspective about the timeline of transformation.

My experience is that transformation is rather like percolation – there's a lot of coughing and spluttering before anything good appears. However, as any coffee lover knows, every drip and every trickle is worth it in the end. This chapter is essentially an exploration of some of the things that have helped make the Eden brew so potent, that is, an attempt to enter the mystery of formation and transformation. We've come far enough in the story already for you to know that involvement in this kind of ministry involves risk and carries a cost – mentally, emotionally, physically and spiritually. Maybe the next few pages will help you to become more alert to those risks, and to prevent these risks turning into realities.

As a common starting point, let's first accept that we don't arrive on the mission-field as the finished article. Most Eden team members spend the first year wrestling with just how inadequate and unprepared they feel, so you're in good company. After all, who are any of us to lay any claim to being agents of transformation? Therefore, even as we're taking our first tentative steps outward toward our neighbourhood we must also start to address our inner state by getting intentional about the nurture of our soul and the growth of our character. Eden has adopted the word 'formation' to describe this process. Unlike information-based approaches to learning, formation can't be a solo pursuit; rather, we grow in community with others. Formation isn't about easy answers but is about wrestling creatively with the complex questions that arise as we pursue the mission of God amongst the people he sends us to. We need to have confidence that as we trust and obey, Christ's image will be formed in us, and will become more and more apparent to those around us.

All or nothing, by Sid Williams

I was once asked to give a talk to an audience of youth workers on the theme of 'All or nothing youth discipleship'. Wow, what an awesome title! But what does it actually mean in real life?

Well, frankly it could look like as many different things as there are young people out there! If I was to claim to have discovered some special formula then I'd be conning you, because there isn't one. But don't get me wrong, I'm not being evasive, I believe that Jesus is immensely practical in the way we see him love people. He preaches what he practices and he only does what he sees the Father doing. Therefore I believe that Eden starts with a heart in us that says, "God, help me love like you love."

My time in Manchester has proved to me that you're better off asking God who he is calling you to, rather than asking what he wants you to do. I've tried lots of 'doing'-related stuff, including both volunteer and paid work for Eden, I've set up and run a social enterprise to get young men into work, I've taken rough lads from the estate to the slums of Nairobi. My point is, all these things have value but the calling is not explicitly to them. The calling is to people, to a community, and to sharing life with that community. God is love and the gospel is God's message to be shared! Keep it simple – love.

Mark offers a perfect example. He's a lad I've known for nearly five years. I didn't meet him through a youth club, instead I bumped into him because he lived just across the road from the house I'd moved into with my friend Keith. After a little while we discovered that behind the broken windows of that small house, Mark slept every night on the cold wooden floor. He shared the house with his six brothers and sisters and their exhausted single mum. They didn't have a bed between them. Yes, that's right, in England, in the twenty-first century, they slept with blankets on the floor.

They were a very secret family, rarely leaving the house which they'd got through a council homelessness scheme. After three months of building trust, Keith and I were finally given the opportunity to enter their home. Once the reality of the situation hit us we knew we couldn't waste any time. We bought them beds to sleep in, helped them work through difficult meetings with school and got on the case with their ever-changing social workers. And we patiently sat through screaming, angry rants from Mum who was hurting from years of abuse. Her deep sorrow sometimes meant that she couldn't function, or took it out on the children. So whilst we knew she wasn't angry with us, we let her vent in our direction, as it seemed to do her some good to get the pain out of her system. Every time we returned she saw that we were really serious about being there for her. No parent or partner or authority figure had shown that before. Love was weird to her.

We had to learn to journey with this family. Meeting them wasn't in our ten-point plan of how to transform the neighbourhood. When we started to get involved we had no idea of the demands that would be placed on us – we were simply seeking to treat this family like we felt Jesus would. God had to work in the hearts of two single young guys to grow in us a long-term commitment that we didn't possess as a natural capacity.

A key moment happened when Mark ran away from home. He was missing for four days and we were all intensely worried. He was eventually found by the police, in Wales, very cold and frightened. He was 15 at the time. But here's what happened next: The police knew us from all the community work we do, so brought Mark to our door and asked us to look after him overnight as the home situation was still very delicate. Eight months later Mark left our house to be reunited with Mum. During that time, we offered him love, shared our home, lost our social lives and any personal space, had to wrestle a knife off him, and dealt with the trouble he got into, often with our other neighbours who didn't like him. And of course we became great friends. One year Keith and

I didn't go home to our families for Christmas but spent it with Mark's family instead. For once in their lives the family experienced a Christmas Day that included a roast dinner and the exchanging of presents. More recently we've even been on holiday together!

Today Mark is 18 and looking for work. His mum believes in a great God's love for her because she's become surrounded by evidence of it. Through a Christian landlord we've managed to rehouse the family and a number of them have started to follow Jesus for themselves. Some of the kids are now outpacing us in our faith – they pray for the sick and see them healed, they love to sing God's praises in church and serve willingly. They're bright and full of fun and recognise God's intervention in their lives. We stay involved with the family, not because we're service providers – they have never trusted service providers – but because they've become our family now.

Church As Mission

At the centre of God's process of our formation is that unique and special community called the church. In earlier chapters of the book I covered some of the challenges that may crop up when the internal priorities of the church are pulling in a different direction to the opportunities unfolding outside of its four walls. I hope that by including some of these struggles I haven't given the impression that church is some kind of obstruction or inconvenience that we'd be better off without. Sadly many people who are passionate about reaching the lost do have that attitude, but I think I can safely say that our Eden teams don't think or act like that. Being church is at the heart of our understanding of what we're all about. We know that our teams of tentmakers would be utterly bereft if it wasn't for the larger fellowship of local believers that they belong to.

One of the most rewarding things about watching Eden grow and flourish in recent years has been to see new freedom and vigour brought to churches that had been experiencing limitations and frustrations. What makes this even more rewarding is the clear evidence that it is the Spirit's work – not ours. We simply don't have a schema when it comes to church. In fact, amongst Eden's leadership we have a sort of unwritten policy that we won't get involved in tinkering with the way our partner churches choose to orient and organise themselves. Our expectation is, though, that if our team members are honouring the church with a share of their time, talents and treasure, then blessing will follow. Whatever the tradition or doctrinal convictions – and there is quite a bit of variance across the network – our teams ought to be a source of life. In summary then, being church is hugely important to Eden, however the thing that holds the Eden Network together is a common missiology, not a common ecclesiology.

Those with a nose for it will detect here the influence of 'Missio Dei' thinking, the branch of theology that traces the initiative for mission back to the Trinity: God's inner life of love is overflowing toward the world, and he invites us to participate in what he's already doing. The deeper meaning of this is entirely consistent with what you'd expect from a movement known for its emphasis on being incarnational. What I mean by that is, equal value is assigned to the body of Christ expressing its external life and to the practices of its internal life. Or in simple terms, sharing a flask of hot chocolate and a biscuit with a group of shivering teenagers in a bus stop on a windy winter evening is as important as sharing a wafer and a cup of grape juice with the congregation on a Sunday morning.

Transformation in Tragedy

Some of the most stunning examples of churches living out their missional potential come in the midst of a profound tragedy. One of the most powerful moments I've known took place in East Manchester in 2010. Like many poor urban communities Openshaw had begun to lose its collective ability to grieve well. Funerals had become toxic affairs often enacted on the street and marked by disputes, disorder and drunken violence. Over the course of about a year the Eden team there, and in particular Sam, the pastor of the Salvation Army church we partner with, had been supporting a young man battling against cancer. This brave teenager, Cody O'Grady, had been involved in the youth work pioneered by the Eden team for many years and his family had received support from the church in lots of ways. When, at the end of a long fight, Cody passed away, the first person his parents called round to the house was Sam. They sat together at the bedside until the doctor and the ambulance arrived.

It was a natural step for them to ask Sam to 'do the funeral' as they had come to call the Salvation Army 'their church'. They wanted everyone to be there, and they had some specific ideas about what might make for fitting tributes to celebrate Cody's life.

First on their list was that the funeral wouldn't be a morbid affair, they'd been to too many of those sort of funerals. To Cody's parents, Steve and Debbie, this translated into a specific dress code – no black and no formal wear – no suits, no frocks. All Cody ever wore was tracksuits so if trackies were good enough for him they were good enough for anyone. Sam promptly nipped down to JD Sports to buy himself a brand-new tracksuit to wear as he presided over the funeral service. Secondly there was the small matter of the wake. This is where things often get messy and as Sam spent time talking with Steve and Debbie it was clear that trouble at the wake would be taken as a huge disrespect to Cody. Together they came up with a genius plan. Milk. In the last few months of his life, due to the numerous medications and treatments he was receiving, Cody wasn't enjoying eating or drinking. The one thing he did enjoy however was a nice glass of ice-cold milk, so that's what everyone would have!

The funeral was a true milestone for the whole community, and for Steve and Debbie it marked a new page in their journey, as Steve explains.

No one messes with 'the Ris', by Steve O'Grady

For me, and my family, Eden has always been there, you're all good guys, you'll always help.

You don't brainwash people with the God stuff, you tell 'em about God and if they wanna listen they listen and if they don't they don't, but they do seem to wanna listen round here because you've made a great difference to the community, because you've stuck it out. It takes a lot to get people's trust round here and you've got it now. They've got respect for you, the kids, and the parents. Openshaw would go under if you guys weren't here.

Through Cody coming to the Eden club and that, I've met some brilliant people, and I really mean that, all the people that have come here, they've changed my life. I've started to get off the drugs now and I'm down to one or two cans a day. You've helped me out no end, when I had all that bad stuff happening with our Cody, when he was in hospital all that long time you were with me. I could phone you at two or three o'clock in the morning. I couldn't even do that with my own family, you know what I mean, but you were there for me.

I can see that God motivates you, he's always there with you, you're always there with him, and you're always here with us. You give your all to it and even more than that as well. It's not all about church on Sundays, you give advice, comfort and even protection for some people. I know that it's not about being rich, it's about being enriched and that's what you've done with me.

No one messes with 'the Ris' – no one; no one messes with 'the Risen Lord' – you can't, can you? He's the man.

Sam isn't alone in being called upon to step up at difficult times like this. Whilst the Eden team members may often be involved behind the scenes the onus will generally be upon the church leaders to provide unity and focus. Many other church leaders have found themselves being the lone voice speaking out hope into broken and fearful hearts, perhaps in the aftermath of a violent gang-related murder or following the loss of a child in a tragic accident. The words and actions conveyed by the church at these times more often than not occur in the space beyond the comfort of the sanctuary. This kind of involvement is extraordinarily important as these events can be hinge moments in the life of a community. The way they're dealt with may serve to either accelerate or slow down community transformation.

Re-understanding Servanthood

In the pressure cooker that community life can so often be there's a danger that the relationships between our team members and the young people and families they're drawn toward may become distorted. Let me explain what I mean. Compassionate ministry often appeals to those who have a need to be needed.

I've sometimes heard this explained using the Mary and Martha story from the gospels, and maybe that goes some way to explaining it. But this is about more than just the fact that some people might be wired to busy themselves whilst others are more inclined towards reclining in the presence of Jesus. What we must realise here is that in any web of human connections there are always power games at work. Be it a family, a workplace, a school, or a community, there will be some kind of pecking order and people will be working out their perceived value in reference to others. This obviously has an influence upon the integrity of our relationships – are we stooping from on high or walking alongside?

The first thing we need to look at is the popular Christian image of the servant. What do we really mean when we throw that word around, or when we attach it to others to create little word combos such as 'servant leadership' or 'servant ministry' or 'servant evangelism'? I'd hazard a guess that the most prevalent mental and emotional connections with that word probably come from one of the following sources.

An obvious starting point is our experience of the service industry – a smiling, helpful greeter in the local supermarket, or the waiter at your table in Pizza Express. Living in a consumer society we tend to have quite a clear idea of what good service ought to look like – and we know when we don't get it! Let's be clear that being a servant in biblical terms has nothing to do with that type of serving. Next, and this applies especially to anyone who has spent any time working in the community sector, is the concept of being a 'service provider'. This label tends to be applied as a blanket term to describe any individual or group that is delivering some sort of project or intervention within a community. The implication is, although it's not always the case, that the service providers have the solutions and they're bringing them into the community, which has the problems.

The difficulty with the first example is that it fosters a certain fakeness within the relationship. The greeter may be very nice and polite to you, but she doesn't really want to know you on any deep level. She's waiting for the shift to end at six o'clock when she can go home to see her boyfriend. Likewise, in ministry, we may find ourselves on the rota to help run a certain activity and yet we don't properly honour the relationship-building opportunities that time affords us. Rather, we may just clock in, go through the motions, being perfectly gracious and kind to everyone, and then clock off again having had nothing but superficial contact. In the service-provider example the issue is that the basis of the relationship is skewed right from the beginning. If those we're reaching out to catch any whiff of superiority from us, or if they feel patronised in any way, then the barriers will go up and that's the end of the line for the development of the relationship. It's fair to say that Eden teams have fallen into both these traps on many occasions but we're learning to do that less and less.

Our own spiritual formation, and the transformation of the communities we've become part of, involves a deeper understanding of what Jesus meant when he used the servant image. Studying the way Jesus employs the servant image in the gospels there appears to be a clear pattern – he either uses the image as a call to obedience, or as a critique of power. Both those things are profoundly counter-cultural in today's world. It's a completely foreign concept now to get on and do something because someone deserving of, and demanding of, our unquestioning allegiance has asked it of us. The same goes for recognising that our society is profoundly unequal, and that in order to put that right we might have to willingly let go of our own power, in situations within which we could quite naturally take control. We may bring expertise into the community but that doesn't give us the right to walk around acting like experts.

Three Little Words

And will it really make any difference if we get this right? Absolutely, it will make the world of difference. One of the things we began to realise as we reflected on the first few years of Eden was that we had unintentionally allowed a whole load of young people and even some of their family members to become dependent on us in various aspects of their life – including their spiritual life. This was immensely draining to the team members, some of whom began to resent the constant demands that were being made on them. It also created a sort of shell around the team, in that those who were coming to Christ and being discipled always remained beyond the inner circle of the team; which was essentially the 'mature Christians' who had moved into the estate. This eventually became a source of real friction until it was outed and dealt with.

These days then we tend to sum up this relational learning in three little words: To, For and With. Each of these words is representative of a particular ministry mindset. The first word, *TO*, takes 'witnessing' as basically something that we do TO other people. We have our gospel product, we know what it looks like, sounds like and smells like, we simply have to tell as many people as possible of its benefits and convince them that they need it in their life. You can immediately see the similarity with the door-to-door salesman.

The second word, *FOR*, treats everyone as an individual, which is a good thing, right? We recognise that the gospel reaches people at their point of need, and so that becomes the way we go about reaching people – doing all sorts of things FOR people, in order that they will have their needs met. As I've already mentioned it's easy to baptise this approach in the language of serving others, and indeed we may genuinely desire to be a blessing. And yet as we've seen already there are some major limitations with this approach too, mainly to do with issues of dependency, and accidentally creating a consumer culture. A good rule of thumb to abide by is never to rob anyone of their dignity by doing something for them that they can be helped to do for themselves.

Finally, *WITH*. If we adopt this mindset then we recognise that following Jesus is a journey that involves growing in companionship with all sorts of people, many who aren't like us one bit. Yes, we may have some special gifts and some important insights that we can share with others, but we recognise that we have flaws and problems too. Therefore, as we pursue the mission of God in our neighbourhood, we open ourselves up to the possibility that we might learn from those we thought we'd be teaching, and may be blessed by those we thought we'd be blessing.

It's not easy to function 100% of our time in the WITH mindset, because doing things TO and FOR those around us comes so easily. And yet we ought to aspire and strive to journey WITH others because this is how true friendship grows. This is one of the most special qualities about living the Eden life – the unlikely friendships that we find ourselves caught up in. A friendship is a genuine two-way street where both people are sharing life's highs and lows together. Perhaps that's why one of the most powerful statements Jesus makes on the subject of servanthood actually places servanthood as a staging post on the way to something even better: "I no longer call you servants, because a servant does not know his master's business. Instead, I have called you friends, for everything that I learned from my Father I have made known to you." *(John 15:15)*

John McGuinness and Ben Woodfield are a fantastic example of what can happen when we choose to journey with someone we're reaching out to, rather than simply offering a service to or for them.

John, on getting to know Ben

The first time I met Ben I was ten years old. He was doing detached street work in Old Trafford and I was on the way to causing trouble, messing about with my mates. Ben started talking to us, telling us about the work that was going on and the things we could get involved in. At first I thought he was weird for approaching us, just coming straight up to us and talking, and when I found out they had moved onto School Walk estate, my neighbouring estate, I thought he was going to get terrored for being a Christian and living there in such a bad estate at the time.

I started to attend the youth club Ben and the Eden team ran on a Monday night, and here they first started to talk to me about Jesus. It was here where I started to get to know Ben. At that time my behaviour was pretty bad. I was getting excluded from school, back-chatting to my mum and causing trouble in my neighbourhood – this behaviour had started because my dad died when I was nine.

Ben invited me to attend his church, I did and I met new people and felt at home and have been part of the church family for four years, where I now play in the band. Since I met

Ben I have calmed down and finished my school education, completed my GCSEs, and I am doing a full-time plumbing course. Ben has mentored me and got me involved in various things around the community, the local housing trust, the Eden project to name a few. Ben has helped me by being there for me. He has helped me grow up into an adult, I am now 17 years old. He has nurtured me with my faith as a Christian. If it wasn't for Ben and the team I think I would be in a pretty bad place now.

Ben, on getting to know John

When John was nine, his dad died. This obviously had a major effect on the whole family. Quickly the feelings of anger and confusion that surround the death of a father intensified in John and began to affect his sense of identity. His actions and attitude changed for the worse and he started making bad choices, getting regular exclusions at school and groundings at home. Barbara, John's mum, a solid and consistent person he has always had in his life, began to wonder how to deal with him.

It was at this point I met John, out on the streets of Old Trafford. These local streets recount stories shared by many other urban neighbourhoods – tainted by crime, gangs, addiction and unemployment. However, as a team and as a church we share the community's anticipation that things can and will get better.

As we got to know him, and he got to know us, John became curious about Jesus and after working through his questions, he chose to become a disciple. This occurred as John began to enter his teenage years, as he also started to realise the consequences his actions were having. John is now 17 years old. He is learning how to follow Christ in a tough world.

I've loved being a mentor to John, meeting him every week and helping him reach towards his goals, like taking his GCSE exams. I'm immensely proud that he's putting the work into gaining a positive future, such as securing a place at Trafford College doing plumbing. I was absolutely thrilled when he won the 'Urban Hero of the Year Award' and had his story featured in the Manchester Evening News.

John's story isn't one of going from being a 'bad' person to a 'good' person, but more a journey of a young lad who has started to make positive decisions in the face of some of life's harder experiences. He is a shining example of following the ultimate role model, Jesus, in an environment where his peers are self-destructing all around. He has a bright future ahead of him and more and more, he is becoming the man God wants him to be.

John has shown me what it means to follow Jesus without losing your heritage, personality and culture. He possesses incredible leadership potential within a lovable extrovert personality. He has taught me what it means to attempt to follow Jesus in a hard place, with intense pressure on his life in various forms. His discipleship helps form my discipleship and it continues to be an honour to know him.

Thin Moments

Finally, no discussion about formation and transformation would be complete if it didn't cover the central devotional disciplines of worship and prayer. All the Eden teams lean heavily on these practices in order to develop the depth of spirituality required for their calling. Eden's calendar year includes events of different shapes and sizes to cultivate a healthy, prayerful culture amongst the teams. There'll often be a very special atmosphere when the teams gather together to focus on praise and intercession. One of the amazing things is that when facing seemingly insurmountable challenges we've lifted up our hearts and voices to God and seen remarkable breakthroughs. There have been times when we have literally been able to pinpoint the precise moment that something permanently shifted.

And yet, we'd suffer a real loss if these events were the only times we encountered God or heard his voice. A key element in the spiritual formation of an Eden team member is the cultivation of the ability to find God in the ordinary – to experience what the Celtic Christians called 'thin' moments, in the midst of the mundane and indeed even the profane. I sometimes refer to this as 'growing gills'. What I mean by that is that in the early stages of someone's time in a challenging urban neighbourhood, many things are new, different and challenging. It can be a bit like swimming underwater when your whole life has been spent walking on dry land. There is the constant need to come up for air – to get out of the neighbourhood – even out of the city – in order to breathe again. Yet over time, as we adjust to our new reality, and in particular as we learn to see beauty amongst ugliness and grace amongst fallenness, our soul is refreshed, oxygenated – right there in the heart of the mess. Our soul grows gills!

This is a process that I've been through personally. Some of my most vivid memories of my time in the draughty old council house in Benchill come from the first winter I spent there. I recall being in a really good devotional rhythm back then, getting up early every morning to pray. My routine was to come downstairs into the lounge, which would be freezing after a chilly night with no double-glazing. I'd turn the gas fire on full and kneel in front of it in a foetal position, letting the heat waft over my head and back. One morning, feeling concerned about the huge commitment I'd made and not knowing what the future held, I whispered to God a prayer seeking reassurance. Right at that instant the gas boiler, which like many council houses of that era was fitted into the chimney alcove behind the fire, let out an almighty WHOOOSH! The central heating thermostat had kicked in to warm the house before my housemates got out of bed.

In that split second of ignition God had answered my prayer with a physical sign saying, "I won't let your heart grow cold. I've fitted you with a thermostat and I'm setting the level. When you begin to sense a chill in your soul my Holy Spirit is going to kick in and you'll feel the fire."

I'm sure that most team members would relate similar experiences and events. Some would speak of dreams in the night, others of visions in the day. One guy was strolling through his neighbourhood at about eight in the evening. He was prayer-walking with members of his home-group enjoying a bit of time with God. Passing one of his friends' houses he looked up into the darkness and was suddenly stunned to see a huge bright angel – wings, sword, the works – sitting up on the apex of the roof and looking around, as if on guard duty. Looking ahead up the street to his left and right he could see other houses occupied by Eden team members. Every single house had an angel, just one, sitting on its roof. All the angels were similar, and yet had slightly unique personal features. All seemed to be charged with the same task – ensuring the special protection of the servants of God. Of all the guys on the team this guy certainly didn't have the reputation of being the 'out-there wacky prophetic one' – quite the opposite really. Perhaps that's why God chose him in particular to peel back the supernatural veil and offer this glimpse into a deeper reality.

And so we see that in the community of the church, in the tumult of life, in the way that we serve and the way that we pray, formation is taking place. That formation, hidden deep in our own souls, is inextricably linked to every outward sign of progress and blessing. I'd venture that, when we can point to both, and make the link, we may be ready to legitimately start using describing what's going on as trans-formation.

CHAPTER EIGHT

GIVING IT AWAY

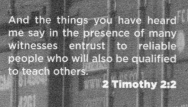

And the things you have heard me say in the presence of many witnesses entrust to reliable people who will also be qualified to teach others.

2 Timothy 2:2

The gospel is good news for sick people and is disturbing for those who think they've got it all together.

Shane Claiborne

Holidays Are Dangerous

Like many people I'm full of good intentions when it comes to aspiring to find space in my busy week to get quality time with God. And like many people, more often than not that simply doesn't happen – or becomes a fleeting moment grabbed between pressing concerns. No, for me, the best times of hearing God come when I get away from all the distractions, the further away the better, ideally well beyond the borders of England altogether!

In the summer of 2004 my wife and I were travelling in Spain. It was before our two boys had arrived on the scene, so holidays then were much more flexible. We were working our way down the coast from the Pyrenees in a little hire car and eventually arrived in one of my favourite cities – Barcelona. I always like to take a few books away with me on trips and this time *Red Moon Rising* by Pete Greig was among them. In the book Pete retells the remarkable story of the global 24-7 Prayer movement. After a long drive we checked in at our hotel and I sat down on the bed to pick up where I'd left off earlier that morning. I'd reached the part of the book where Pete describes pretty much having had enough of the whole thing. As he tells it, he confided in a close friend that he was considering closing down 24-7 Prayer. Thankfully his friend persuaded him not to make any hasty decisions. It was good advice that created the space for God to speak afresh into the situation. Over the next few days Pete heard God telling him that the 24-7 initiative was divine in both origin and oversight, and the decision to end it wasn't something he'd been given authority to take.

As I read the story I was impacted by the remarkable similarity with Eden. I don't mean that I was fed up, quite the opposite. However, I was probably beginning to overstep the mark and starting to believe, if only subtly and subconsciously, that Eden was my responsibility. For reasons I didn't fully understand at the time, God wanted to underline to me that the initiative for Eden was, and remained, his. Guys like me and Andy had simply been afforded the privilege of stewarding the thing, but we shouldn't kid ourselves that we owned it. In the days ahead as I prayed and sought to press deeper into this revelation I began to sense why God had brought it to my attention. The reason could be summed up in a single phrase that was ringing in my ears by the time I boarded the plane to return to Manchester: 'Give it away.'

And so it was with some trepidation that I came back to the office after that fortnight away. Knowing that the first thing I needed to do was to convey to Andy all that I thought God had been saying to me, my head was full of scraps of conversation that were forming a loose script. I kicked back in my chair to open a couple of weeks' worth of post as all this spun around my mind. Behind me was the window and as I opened a padded envelope a ray of light caught the shiny surface of the CD that was contained inside it. I almost threw it straight in the bin, assuming it was just another dodgy demo CD – I used to get lots in those days as I was still quite involved in organising events. Thankfully I took a second look at it. Stuffed into the envelope was a hand-written letter from someone I vaguely knew and whose name now escapes me. The gist of it was, "Matt, we recently had a visiting speaker at our church and I really felt that for some reason I ought to send the message to you." I flipped over the CD and read the writing scrawled on the disk in black marker pen. The title of the message was 'Give it away'!

Buoyed up by this unexpected confirmation of the word I felt I'd received whilst in Spain, I went out for lunch with Andy at a local pub. To give credit where it's due Andy, despite having a reputation for being totally tunnel-vision for Manchester, was really open to the idea. He concurred that it really sounded to him like God might be opening up a new door for Eden. Recognising that the two of us couldn't just make a bilateral decision there and then, we decided to do a bit of low-key consulting with the numerous other stakeholders in the whole Eden venture. After seeking the counsel of our trustees we gained much greater clarity on what we ought to do next. They've been around long enough to know that having a vision to do something new is the easy part – *how* you put it into action can be much more tricky. In this instance 'Give it away' didn't mean 'Throw it away'; rather, this seemed to be about *entrusting* Eden to a much wider network of partners, across a much wider geography. And we were pretty sure that God would bring people to us that we'd be able to trust with this special commission.

Divine GPS

The Bible says that 'God is not slow in keeping his promises' but goes on to add 'as some understand slowness'. Two years after the events I've just described took place we were no closer to becoming a national network and I was starting to get frustrated – my understanding of 'slowness' clearly needed to come into line with God's! All the necessary adjustments had been made to my diary – I was deliberately trying to get out more beyond the boundaries of Manchester but nothing was happening. Carrying the vision felt like a long hike up a steep hill. I was beginning to fall prey to doubts, wondering whether I'd imagined the whole thing.

Quite out of the blue Andy was contacted by a long-standing friend now based in the States, Mike Breen. Mike had been one of our trustees some years ago, knew our vision well, and always acted as a great encouragement to us. He wanted to offer us the opportunity to get involved in a new initiative he was planning together with an American group called Leadership Network. Their dream was to gather churches and ministries from across Europe, selected according to their reputation for stretching the boundaries of mission and for getting results. The emphasis of the gathering would be to stimulate a new wave of creative church-planting right across Europe. After initially declining the invitation on the basis that we're not church planters we were challenged to broaden our definition of what church-planting actually is – with particular reference to Eden's success in growing Christian community in places lacking any formalised expression of church. And so we accepted the invitation to participate and awaited further details arriving.

A few months later, in February 2007, the first ECPN gathering began. Here we were, amongst an eclectic bunch from all over Europe that brought the silver hair of Sandy Millar from Holy Trinity Brompton alongside the studded noses of the Jesus Freaks from Germany. It was truly humbling to be in the company of leaders and pioneers of the highest calibre. The style of the event – called a Learning Community – was unlike anything we'd encountered before. Yet beyond all this something deeper was stirring in me that had more to do with the place than the people. We were gathered in Barcelona, literally just down the street from the hotel I'd been staying in when God had first quickened my spirit with the 'Give it away' vision! It was as if a divine GPS had brought me back to the spot in order to remind me and stir my faith again. These gatherings, which were to take place every six months for the next four years, were to prove absolutely critical in our process of working out how to give Eden away, and to whom.

Hope and Fears

We'd known for a long time that people in other cities were interested in the Eden model of community ministry. Once we even received a delegation from South Africa who practically begged us to help them launch Eden in their city. Like the dozens of other times when we'd been asked the same question before, we politely but firmly explained that our calling was to bring transformation to communities much closer to home. 'We're called to Manchester' had been our mantra for so long that beginning to visualise developing our work in other cities was actually very difficult. We knew that we couldn't just manufacture Eden carbon copies, therefore what should we class as non-negotiable and what could we be more flexible about? It was also quite disconcerting to be faced with the challenge of going to places that we didn't really know and where we weren't well known. When you've been used to operating in a certain environment, and you know that place well, and you've developed a bit of respect and reputation, it feels weird to turn up somewhere that people haven't got a clue who you are. It's also really healthy though – a great antidote to any egotism.

Amongst our leadership the overriding concern seemed to be that in the very act of giving Eden away we might also be condemning it to death by dilution. How could we be sure that an Eden team based in a North Eastern seaport would have any similarity to an Eden team squeezed in around the back of a busy London train station? And how would either of those contexts relate to the already established Eden teams around the old docks in Salford or standing in the shadows of the great red-brick mills of Oldham? The question really boiled down to what we began to call 'maintaining a family likeness'. Our sense was that the common leadership phraseology of 'shared

DNA' didn't quite go far enough. If DNA is an invisible structure that enables life, then we needed to define what that life could, should and would look like. Even across considerable distances we'd have to work hard at cultivating some kind of common life. We'd need to communicate with one another – and actually spend time in each other's company – even if it cost in terms of time and money.

Ultimately, driving us forward was the conviction that an Eden team will make a profound difference within any poverty-afflicted neighbourhood. If we could adhere to the principles we'd learned – of investing in passionate leaders, of carefully selecting team members who would be in for the long haul, and of helping these amazing people to live prayerfully, relationally and missionally, then we'd see transformation. On top of this, there has been a strong sense of growing toward a certain tipping point. Nobody quite knows where that point will come – whether it will be at 20, 30, 40, 50 Eden teams? But a day will come when critical mass is achieved and suddenly the movement begins to accelerate all by itself. Instead of going out recruiting, people will be coming to us. Instead of going out fundraising, money will start flowing in. And instead of writing books like this to share the stories of what God is doing, it will become headline news.

Over the Pennines

Amongst the Brits participating in the ECPN gatherings were the leaders of the St Thomas' group of churches in Sheffield. We already knew each other to a degree and as fellow Northerners we naturally found ourselves drawn even more closely together, both through friendly banter but also by our shared passion to bring kingdom transformation to our troubled cities. Paul Maconachie who leads St Thomas', Philadelphia (now called

Network Church Sheffield) was especially keen for us to consider bringing Eden over the hills to Sheffield. Paul has a strong prophetic gift and we sensed a real agreement in our own spirits that this was the invitation we'd been waiting for. Diaries were organised and a date was set for Andy and me to come and spend a day in Sheffield. Our objective was to begin to discern whereabouts within that great city of half a million souls we might establish an Eden team.

Sheffield really is quite unique, mainly because it manages to combine being extraordinarily hilly with being extremely industrial. Why on earth such a big city exists in such an awkward location is utterly baffling. The views from any one of the many steep inclines show a patchwork of large factories and terraced streets now broken by more modern high-rise developments – some flashy and new, many dated and depressing. In many ways Sheffield has been playing catch-up with Britain's other major cities. It was hit doubly hard back in the eighties by the decline of both the steel and the coal industries. In recent years economic regeneration had begun to gain traction but the credit crunch brought an end to much of that development, meaning that many signs of industrial decay still remain littered around the landscape of the city.

It was a chilly and drizzly Northern morning when Andy and I were bundled into a rattly minibus and given an alternative tour of Sheffield by the guys from St Tom's and some of their friends from around the city. Our itinerary had at least half a dozen communities on it and in every place we touched down there was a warm welcome for us from Christians already based there. We drank lots of tea and asked lots of questions hoping that we might latch on to something extra, something special that might help us to set apart one place from another. One thing was without question – Sheffield clearly had some incredibly needy communities and Eden really ought to be a part of the response. As we reflected at the end of the day over a cup of strong coffee things started to make sense.

One of the places we'd visited was a large estate a couple of miles to the south east of the city centre. We'd been introduced to the local Anglican ministers there, an earnest and energetic couple called Jasper and Tina Hodges. Their parish, which covered a vast swathe of low-rise council housing from the forties and fifties, has one of the most convoluted names I've ever come across. Thankfully Jasper and Tina chose to abbreviate it to 'The Beacon', a name that fits well with the location of their church centre – a renovated pub. The Beacon sits prominently on the main road that separates the two neighbourhoods they serve, Arbourthorne and Norfolk Park. In the brief time we had together a number of things had become apparent. The local area, whilst not having all the immediate visual signs of deprivation, had a very high population of children, youth and young parents. A large proportion of these were living in homes entirely funded by welfare benefits. It was obvious that Jasper and Tina possessed a profound compassion for the residents of the community. As two very capable ordained clergy they could have easily opted for a well-heeled parish that would make far fewer demands on them but here they were pursuing the gospel of good news to the poor. The potential to accelerate their work by partnering together to form an Eden team was clear and so that's exactly what we agreed to do.

Home is where the heart is, by Tracey

A year and a half ago I hated life, and I didn't want to live. I felt God was 10 million miles away and that no matter what anyone did to me, I couldn't possibly hurt any more. I felt alone and depressed which led to me self-harming.

Communication in my family broke down which meant I felt more and more alone. I didn't feel I had many friends I could talk to about the stuff that was going off at home. It seemed to get worse when I became a teenager – life seemed to be continually hurtful.

I felt like I had to be 30 even though I was only 13. I struggled with feeling responsible for situations that had happened in my family life. I started to get angrier the more hurt I got.

Things continued to get more difficult at home. It got to a point where I was no longer able to live at home. When I was 14 my mum had to go into hospital which meant that my brother, sister and I had to find somewhere to live temporarily until my mum was able to come back. I went to live with various people, and didn't go straight back home when she was out of hospital. When I thought things had improved at home, I went back, but if anything, things felt worse. Communication was still difficult and strained, and it felt like we were always arguing. I tried my best to make things work at home, but events that happened made me think that it would be better for my family relationships if we lived apart.

At one point I had nowhere to live, and that was when my Eden team leader and his family took me in for two months. While I lived with them I started going back to church. People were talking to me about God and his love for me but because I was feeling so hurt I found it hard to accept. I wondered why things had to be so difficult if God was on my side. Why did everything bad seem to be happening in my life?

Although I knew I was always welcome in my Eden leader's house, I knew that staying with them permanently wasn't an option, as they physically didn't have enough room for me. When I realised this I approached the church leaders – they had let me stay with them for a little while when my mum was in hospital, and so I wondered if I could live with them longer term. They told me that they needed time to think and pray about it. Although I didn't have much faith at the time, I couldn't help but hope that their answer would be yes.

Through going back to church week after week, part of me was opening up to what people were trying to tell me: that God had complete control over my situation and wanted it resolved. After consideration, the church leaders said I could return to live with them, and although the transition was challenging, living with them has helped me grow further with my faith, and their encouragement kept me on God's path.

My life was changing for the better but I was still hurting and self-harming because of stuff going on. Some family members found my choice of living arrangement hard to accept. Although my trust for people had been broken in the past, I felt like I could talk more about my issues. I am not saying this was easy because it wasn't, but without talking it only made me feel worse and that's when I felt the need to self-harm.

I am now 16 and the situation is improving. I feel more confident in myself and my faith through the help and support of the Eden team and my church family and friends. Things aren't perfect, but I'm learning that dealing with my situation on my own is not the best way, and that with God's help I can find the best solutions. Even though things are still difficult with my natural family, things have started to improve a little and the way I now look at the situation is more positive. I now know with God 'I can do all things though Christ who strengthens me!' (Philippians 4:13)

Proper Yorkshire

My dad's a Yorkshireman and I have quite a lot of relatives living over that side of the Pennines, so I know a thing or two about the place and its culture. Perhaps if you're familiar with Yorkshire you'll recognise the paradox that I'm about to describe. The thing is, on the one hand there are few regions in England that cling so tightly to their identity – being 'Yorkshire' is a real badge of honour. And yet at the same time there are few regions in England that have such fierce rivalries between neighbouring towns and cities. Bradford is a classic example. Bradford residents would be exceedingly proud of their proper Yorkshire credentials, and yet there's no love lost between Bradford and Leeds, or Wakefield, or Huddersfield, not to mention Sheffield, which might as well be 'in the South' as far as those north of the M62 are concerned.

Bradford is about 40 miles from Manchester, about the same as Sheffield, but it takes half the time to get there as there's door-to-door motorway (while getting to Sheffield involves using the slow, winding lanes over the moors). Our connection to this part of Yorkshire came about through quite an unusual set of circumstances. We've always enjoyed a great relationship with leaders in the New Wine network of churches. Their passion for mission and openness to the work of the Holy Spirit has always made us feel very much at home in their company. In 2009 we were asked to lead a special venue at the New Wine North event. The leaders of New Wine in the North, Ian and

Nadine Parkinson, wanted it to have a really grassroots urban feel – to be pacey, funny and above all to be welcoming and accessible to the many people attending New Wine North who belonged to inner-city and estate churches. We were delighted to be asked and immediately jumped at it.

That week on site in Newark really was something special, and we've been returning to play a part in that festival every year since. The venue was absolutely rammed with people; our crazy mix of worship, comedy, Bible teaching and alternative prayer ministry seemed to be hitting the spot. Andy Hawthorne was given a preaching slot in the main venue on one of the midweek evenings. It was the night that the main offering would be taken and we'd already agreed that all of the money raised would go towards planting Eden teams across the North of England. Obviously we were keen to get an estimate of what would normally be raised in such an offering. We were told that £20,000 would be doing really well and that got us all pretty excited. Andy preached his heart out and as well as doing a great job of sharing the Eden vision he also invited people forward to accept Christ – which many did. Towards the end of the meeting we noticed a flutter of excitement amongst the New Wine leaders. One of the stewards had appeared bearing a piece of paper, with the figure for the offering count written on it. The venue absolutely exploded with praise when Ian announced that over £60,000 had been raised! This meant that we could accelerate our plans for extending Eden across Yorkshire, and there was one guy in particular that we'd been spending time with during the week who we sensed God was joining our hearts with.

Ironically, given all I've said about the curious relationships that exist between the towns and cities in Yorkshire, Stuart Gregg hails from Leeds, yet for 15 years has been pastor of Buttershaw

Baptist Church in Bradford. He's also actively involved in New Wine's own Urban Priority Forum, so we connected quickly regarding the highs and lows of trying to grow vibrant churches within council estate communities. Keen to get a better sense of his turf I took a day trip to Buttershaw a few months later. My first glimpse of the church building told me a great deal. I spend a lot of my time in deprived neighbourhoods and see many different church buildings in these contexts. The first thing I look for are the signs of openness or defendedness. I could take you to churches up and down the country that are hiding behind high fences and barbed wire, churches that have reinforced their doors and bricked up their windows. At Buttershaw Baptist I didn't see any of those things. Here was a well-kept building, sitting behind a low wall, with a lovely colourful sign that looked as if local kids had been involved in making it. The message was simple: here's a church that is well connected within its community. OK, I'm sure over the years there must have been incidents, but on the whole communities don't lay siege to churches they respect – to churches that they know are there for them – churches that are not just located in the community but are actually part of the community.

We spent the next hour or so walking the streets. Like many Northern overspill estates the sense of isolation and stagnation was almost tangible. The sad little parade of empty shops in the centre of the estate is a truly depressing sight. Yet amidst the dereliction it was apparent that improvements were happening slowly, some new houses had been built and many of the existing houses had been recently improved. There was something else about that walk that made it a particularly bittersweet experience. It was sweet because every five minutes we would stop as Stuart was greeted by someone going about their business. It was bitter as, after a few minutes chatting they would walk on, and Stuart would tell me a little of their life story – stories of abuse, neglect, chronic health problems and addictions. Even though I've been involved in Eden for 15 years and have heard those kinds of stories thousands of times, they break my heart every time. I also listened to Stuart describe his passion to reach the youth of the estate, and his frustration that their great kids' work wasn't feeding into an equally great youth work. We sensed that this presented a great opportunity for partnership, and Eden Buttershaw was conceived.

Overcoming the lack, by Stuart Gregg

Inner-city ministry is a gift from God for those convinced of the biblical imperative to the poor and marginalised, which I believe should be everybody! Over twenty years of working in and around Buttershaw estate in South Bradford have convinced me of that. They've also convinced me that such ministry can be incredibly rewarding – 'real people, real problems, real change' is how we phrase it. Unfortunately I'm also sure that there can be huge pressures and costs associated with such work. In particular there are two common challenges: a lack of companions, and a lack of resources.

I often call the lack of companions 'The Elijah Syndrome'. It's the dreadful feeling that 'I am the only one'. I network with a lot of ministers in urban priority areas and at times we all find that the work can be isolating. Struggling against systems and organisations and being a lone voice for change in what are often small traditional churches can start to wear you down. In the early days of working at Buttershaw, constantly being the first to arrive and the last to leave meant life could be hard physically and emotionally. After one of our 'seeker' events that had involved a long day I remember soaking in the bath wondering if it was really worth it. Maybe it was the overstimulation of the day, or perhaps wondering how we would afford the £275 to replace the broken video projector bulb... either way I recall a sleepless night.

The very real lack of resources in urban contexts compounds things, council estates and urban neighbourhoods aren't known for drawing great tithers! In real terms this means that attempts to bring the vision of the church into reality may well falter.

So I know from personal experience how hard it is to keep going in the face of these things!

After a number of years of transition Buttershaw Baptist became an outward-looking community-based church with a heart for sustained mission, relationship building and community engagement. Our social project and a sustained programme of community events meant we were well connected on our estate. A deliberate policy to recruit 'scaffolders' had started to alleviate some of the resources issues, and a number of these wonderful people moving either into or near the area had got the church to the point of sustainability, and brought some growth. However, we still had more ideas than resources. A particular area of concern was that whilst we were making good progress in connecting to local families our youth work was pretty scarce, despite having one couple who were passionate about this vital area.

I clearly remember receiving an email from Matt whilst away on holiday. Once my wife had finished remarking on my lack of wisdom in reading email on holiday, we both got very excited at Matt's request to come and meet us. We'd heard that things were changing for Eden and that there was now a chance to connect with the work that had been established in Manchester. This was a big step forward from the time nearly ten years earlier when I, as a young deacon in the church, had phoned The Message to enquire about Eden coming 'over the border' to Yorkshire. At that time I was given a very definite 'no'.

God's timing is always perfect and our connection to the Eden Network over the last couple of years has benefited Buttershaw immensely. Knowing there are others who share the same heart for the urban poor and who have raised the profile of such work on a national level has brought new confidence and new relationships. Our team is still small and most have been redeployed from within the existing church, so the need for recruitment is pressing, but we have seen immense success. Building on the church's existing relationships, reputation and values has given the Eden team a great springboard.

Our regular timetable now includes free-running, music groups, dance groups, discipleship meetings, and youth cafés and is vastly increasing the number of relationships with estate families, which has in turn had a massive effect on our mission. The joy of celebrating one of our young people as Urban Hero of 2011 lifted the spirits of the church and estate.

Eden is now core to who we are as a church. Not only does it give us wider connection and resources, it has also given us the chance to learn to be generous and to give away what the Lord has given to us.

A Barrier Broken

By the close of 2008 then, the barrier had well and truly been broken – we'd finally launched teams outside of Manchester and there was no way back. In some ways it felt like beginning all over again, with an accompanying sensation that felt a bit like the stage fright that bands experience when they start playing bigger venues. This was what we'd been hoping for and working towards for years and we were immensely grateful to God for the way he'd helped us make the leap.

With a whole new horizon in view it was possible to start translating ideas about becoming a national network from the drawing board and into reality. Now we could do more than merely theorise, we could actually test out how Eden would translate into new contexts. I knew that I needed to make adjustments in my own working life in order to focus properly on the new opportunities. Some of this was just psychological – sticking a coloured heat-map of UK deprivation on my office wall and retraining my mind to think nationally. Some of it was practical: I needed to hand over responsibility for the existing Manchester-based teams to someone with a safe pair of hands. As the doors to other cities began to swing wide open I needed capacity to respond. At some point the biggest door of all, the door to the capital, would start to creak on its ancient hinges, an exciting and a daunting prospect. As yet, though, we had no idea how that would happen.

CHAPTER NINE

CROSS-ROADS OF THE WORLD

Should I not be concerned about that great city?

Jonah 4:11

The most vigorous forms of community are those that define themselves as a group with a mission that lies beyond themselves – thus initiating a risky journey... All great missionary movements begin at the fringes of the church, among the poor and the marginalised.

Alan Hirsch

Pincer Movement

The ECPN Learning Community made it possible for Andy and me to get away for a few days of focused planning and prayer a couple of times a year. These times together helped us to see the things in our operating model that needed to be adapted and improved. Our relationships with the other groups on the church-planting journey with us were deepening too. One of the groups that we were spending a lot of our downtime with was the team from HTB – not only was their vision inspiring, they were great fun to hang out with too. One of the things that really impressed me was their earnest desire to see the gospel of Jesus bring about social transformation, especially in London.

I discovered that after handing over HTB to Nicky Gumbel, Sandy Millar hadn't gone into retirement at all. Instead he'd moved to an inner-city parish in North London, in the shadow of the Emirates Stadium and Finsbury Park mosque. Although well into his sixties and having accomplished pretty much everything a Christian minister could ever hope to, he was still full of passion to see the kingdom come. He invited me to spend a couple of days with him in Tollington Park in Islington. It was an intense experience, a really hectic place, a cultural melting pot like I hadn't witnessed up North. They had a large council estate literally right on the doorstep of their church, St Mark's. The neighbourhood had attracted some notoriety after Tory MP Ann Widdecombe had made a TV programme about it. Over a 'wee dram' late one evening, Sandy asked me whether there might be the possibility of Eden working with his church to establish a missional community in the estate. I remember saying that perhaps at some time in the future we might be able to do that. But at the time we'd hardly got the new projects in Sheffield and Bradford off the ground. Bringing Eden to London felt a long way off.

In February 2009 Andy and I travelled to Portugal for another ECPN gathering. Mike Breen was on particularly fine form, perhaps because he and the rest of his team had decided to colour co-ordinate their outfits, in various pastel shades! As the saying goes, we were 'cooking on gas'; the whiteboards on which we were working out our next wave of strategy were covered in all sorts of scribble and doodles. At the end of the three days we shared our latest dreams in a presentation session with the other teams. When our five-minute slot was over there was a huge cheer and everyone gathered around us to saturate our plans in prayer. Mick Woodhead, one of the leaders from St Thomas' in Sheffield, brought us a really powerful prophetic word. It was a real goosebump moment.

Our return flight to Manchester was scheduled for later that day so we took advantage of a free hour and decided to head down to one of the beach bars to get some food and finally get some sun on our faces after being shut in the hotel all week. As we were sitting down at a table Ric, Miles and Kate from HTB walked in too. We waved them over, rearranged the chairs and started to order some food. Ric wasted no time in turning the conversation towards Eden. Like Sandy, Ric had also left the large, dynamic HTB base church in Kensington in order to breathe new life into a terminal urban church in a deprived community. He'd gone east, to Shadwell in Tower Hamlets, and in just a few years was starting to see real breakthrough. Looking Andy straight in the eye he said, "We need Eden in London, Andy. And we need you to send someone make it happen."

Andy responded immediately: "Well that's great, Ric, we'd love to have Eden in London too, but the only person who could head up a job that big is Matt, and you'll never get him to leave Manchester."

Suddenly all eyes were on me. I was glad I was wearing sunglasses as I have a useless poker face and I was trying really hard not to give anything away. "Funny you should say that, Andy," I replied, "because I was just saying to Frank in the bar last night that if we're really going to see Eden fulfil its potential we need to get it established in London." I think I may have stammered a little at this point as I tried to get my tongue around the next few words. "And I said that I'd probably have to leave Manchester for a while to make sure that it gets off to the best possible start."

My next thought was, "How on earth is my wife going to react to this hare-brained idea?"

On the move again, by Alex Hall

I've been part of two Eden teams and they have been wildly different experiences.

When my husband Phil and I were looking to join Eden Arbourthorne we were about to get married and would be officially joining the project straight after our honeymoon. Having been students we weren't necessarily that fussy about where we lived but had a little wish list that included a garden for growing veggies, a good shower and a gas hob. The only house available on the estate when we needed it was a typical Arbourthorne house, which had a massive garden full of blackberries (one of the many skills I've learnt whilst on Eden is jam-making), the most amazing shower I have ever had in my life and a gas hob. The provision of our little blue house was the clearest 'yes' we needed when asking if this was the right move!

Moving to London was a different story. No perfect little house, but amazing friends. We lived with the vicar and his family for a month (squeezing our two-bed house into one and a half rooms) before a new friend from church, Colin, bought an ex-squat in the middle of the Eden estate at auction. He invited us into the adventure of reclamation and restoration and for the past nine months we've lived amongst builders, brick dust and tools as Phil and Colin have worked on the house. The garden had been a rubbish site for years, the hob was non-existent (no real kitchen for the first five months) and the shower was horrible. The house is almost finished now and will be stunning but the real provision was the friendships we gained by living there, both with church members and the neighbours on the street who came to help and hang out.

Such different experiences but God was completely providing what we needed in both.

Reading the City

The months following my return from Portugal were marked by one door after another opening in London, and one door after another closing in Manchester. Grace, my wife, was suddenly made redundant, and shortly afterwards we found out she was pregnant with our second child. Funding began to flow in anticipation of the new work, which was a great encouragement. Despite living in a decent-sized three-bedroom house in Manchester we knew that we could only afford a small flat in London. When our first child was born we were living on the seventh floor of an apartment block which was no fun at all when the lift was out of action. Grace's only request therefore was that we must find a ground-floor pad. I wanted to be close to a Tube line so that I could easily zip around London. Incredibly we found a nice little place that ticked both boxes, in fact we couldn't have been closer to the Tube – it rattled right past our back window, every five minutes!

The first few months in London were fantastic. I became a ferocious networker and covered a huge number of miles criss-crossing the city from north to south and east to west. I made it my business to do everything I could to absorb London from every angle. My favourite angle was from altitude. I soon discovered that many of the high-rise towers – the notorious sixties 'streets in the sky' – have now been fitted with secure entranceways that you need a key fob to get through. Yes, it's a little bit naughty, but I did become something of an expert at tailgating residents in order to gain entry to the block. Sometimes the smell that greeted me in the lifts made me wish I'd stayed outside, but generally the view from the top would make it all worthwhile. I also followed up the most tenuous of contacts in order to take pulse readings for dozens and dozens of different communities. I loved to grab the local free papers from different parts of the city, checking out what was making it into the news, looking at the price of properties in the sort of neighbourhoods where Eden might find itself located someday. Gradually I began to build up a composite picture in my mind and started to see how Eden might be able to add something of value to the great things that were already going on.

Of course, Eden continued to grow in the cities of the North too during this time and it was on my trips back to places like Sheffield and Bradford that the uniqueness of the London estates began to stand out. There are parts of the North where you would need to buckle up tight in a fast car and drive for quite some time before you leave the poverty behind you. In many parts of London, especially inner London, you just need to cross the street to be in an altogether different world. To put it politely, the close proximity of the rich and poor in London is something of a social idiosyncrasy. To quote the London Evening Standard, it's 'shameful.' Six months into my time in the city they ran a week-long exposé that opened with these words:

"London is a shameful tale of two cities. In the richest capital in Europe almost half our children live below the poverty line. These families are cut off from the life most Londoners take for granted. They are the dispossessed."

Whilst tending towards sensationalism, *the Evening Standard*'s campaign carried a lot of truth. My own conclusion was that London's overlapping worlds simply don't even see each other. It's like a veil of blindness exists that means the same pavements are shared but the people are walking right through one another.

Redefining Impossible

Beyond these initial observations a number of issues were becoming apparent that bore a more direct challenge to Eden's mode of mission. First amongst these was the housing shortage. In the capital there's hardly a square inch that isn't being used by someone. What a contrast to the cities of the North where whole streets sit empty and boarded up. Here even the estates with the shabbiest housing stock and the worst reputations for vice and violence were horrendously overcrowded and overpriced. As I talked to people about Eden's vision of creating incarnational missional communities on these estates it wasn't unusual for me to simply get the response, "It's impossible. You'll have to rethink that part of your strategy."

Looking back now I'm glad that I stubbornly refused to back down on that point; in the first year of the Eden teams commencing their ministry in London we recruited and relocated 19 people into four different estates. That's not a bad result for an impossible task. I mustn't take the glory for that though, those 19 Eden team members are the ones paying the rent every month and it's often a real stretch for them to make ends meet. We still need to see some major breakthroughs in order to be able to source more affordable housing on the estates for our teams. I've even been badgering the government about it – something has to give.

On one occasion I was having coffee with a Baptist minister who I'd been told would be on my wavelength. As our conversation unfolded I asked him whether he had any reflections on the transience that I'd been noticing in many of the estates. After all, what's the point of striving to do long-term incarnational ministry if after five years the residents in your neighbourhood have turned over half a dozen times? His response was well-observed and extremely helpful. "Many inner London estates will split into thirds," he said. "One third are the revolving-door tenants, they'll be in and out in six months. The next third are a bit more stable, perhaps sticking around from two to five years, often for the length of a steady job, until it comes to an end. Finally there are the long-termers, they've been in the community for generations, they have the connections and the memories; they're like gold."

It was obvious that Eden would need to be extremely flexible to adapt to the missional challenge of a fast-moving world city. Tactics that had been tried and tested over years in the North would need reinventing. We're used to working in tight-knit communities, places where you get funny looks as you walk down the street if you're new to the area. We've learned to turn this to our advantage. When a team member moves into their house up North the curtains will be twitching and the kids will be hanging around the removal van wanting to find out who the newbies on their street are. In London people come and go so quickly that the opportunity to get to know people just isn't quite the same. This therefore puts an additional onus on the London teams to be highly proactive in making themselves known to their new neighbours.

Community ~~Fight~~ Fun Day, by Jamie Sewell

We had been living on Lancaster West for about month and our church, Latymer Christian Fellowship, had been organising a Community Fun Day since before we had arrived.

My wife Becci and I were really excited about getting our faces out in the community and meeting new people. LCF had also arranged for a local youth centre to come to the fun day to facilitate some activities for the youth.

After 30 minutes of the barbecue we realised the youth centre weren't coming and the role as games organiser fell to me! In any other circumstance this role is one I'd relish, but due to the unexpected nature of my appointment I found myself ill-prepared. In fact I had no equipment at all.

There was a group of lads hanging around with a football so I had a word with them and they agreed to take part in a 'friendly' kick about; I then explained that we would need to use their football. I gathered another group of lads from around the BBQ area, threw down a few jumpers as goal posts and away we went! I felt very proud of myself – I'd managed to gather over a dozen teenagers for what was proving to be a good game of football. For the following 20 minutes we had a great time and I was feeling pretty smug.

Suddenly, there was a goal dispute, and I found myself in the middle of a very volatile situation. Two lads from each of the different groups were in each other's faces arguing and one was adamant that the only way to settle things was with a fight! I positioned myself in the middle of them and attempted to explain that this was a community FUN day and that we didn't want to fight. To which the main aggressor replied, "But I want to fight!" Before I could do anything else I was engulfed by both groups, each standing behind the person they had an allegiance to. I was jumping in the way of swinging hands desperately trying to stop anyone from being hit.

My attempts to talk the situation down were falling on deaf ears and by this time the lads had started getting out their phones and ringing older brothers to come downstairs from the high-rise flats that surrounded us on every side. In the background I could see the community police officers taking photos with children in masks whilst tucking into a free burger. I was feeling pretty desperate for help that didn't appear to be coming. My first Community Fun Day was going to turn into a Community Fight Day!

Just as I was losing faith in my ability as a human shield separating the angry youths, the police arrived. They'd eventually noticed the situation and came across to find out what was happening. I'd spoken earlier with the main aggressor, and he'd told me that he was 'on tag' for previous crimes. This information gave me a bit of leverage and so I told him that if he didn't chill out he'd be taken off tag and be put back in prison. The tactic worked and he quickly popped up his hood and walked away.

Reflecting later I was struck by how normal this was to so many of the lads. The hostility had gone from 0 to 60 in about ten seconds and yet in the aftermath it was as if nothing had happened. It confirmed to me that round here reputation means everything – even those who hadn't wanted to fight refused to back down because they feared losing face.

The Cross-Cultural Challenge

It's hard to imagine how we might achieve the kingdom transformation we seek in our nation's cities without engaging with the ethnic and cultural differences that exist at the grass roots. Given that Eden has been on the front foot of mission since the nineties we've had a bit of experience in this area. The first few estates we became established in were almost entirely White British in heritage but soon we began to deploy teams into communities that were much more mixed in terms of both race and religion. That said, I'd be the first to admit that we're still in the early stages of our learning in this area.

Establishing new teams in London has been exciting because it's already started to accelerate our understanding in this vital niche of ministry. Many of the young people and families we're getting to know on the Andover Estate in Tollington are fairly recent arrivals from both East and West Africa, as well as many more who are second, third or even fourth generation of Caribbean heritage. The Lincoln estate in Bow has such a large proportion of Bengali residents that the local signage is printed in Bangla as well as English. The Lancaster West and the Dalgarno, both estates in North Kensington, are incredibly diverse with dozens of nationalities represented.

Related to this is the question of the cultural identity of our teams – where are we coming from? Perhaps because like attracts like, or maybe due to the fact that most of our recruiting has historically been done at big summer Christian festivals like

Soul Survivor and New Wine, our teams have been mainly white Caucasian in complexion. Again, coming to London presented a great opportunity to improve the balance of our teams so that they might begin to better reflect the varied heritages present in our communities. My experience has been that until you turn an aspiration into a goal it will never get done, so concrete steps needed to be taken. With London being the only city in the nation where there are more non-white Christians than white Christians we had a chance to get to know, and hopefully recruit from, new networks of passionate, growing and outward-looking black churches.

The first step was to recruit someone to the Eden London board of trustees who could bring a depth of insight to these challenges. I'd already invited John Sutherland to be on the board as in the years since first visiting me in Manchester we'd become great friends. He'd immediately and enthusiastically accepted my invitation. Johnny was a good guy to talk to about this because the many promotions he's received in the Met now place him in a position where he has a remarkable bird's eye view of who's who in London. I asked him who else could join us to bring this missing dimension. The first name off his lips was Nims Obunge, director of the Peace Alliance, a seriously well-networked guy of Nigerian descent. I asked Johnny to set up a meeting between Nims and myself and a few weeks later I found myself at 'Freedom's Ark' in Tottenham wondering what to expect. I'd been waiting for a few minutes when Nims flew in through the door at a hundred miles an hour. On the surface of it everything seemed good – smiles, warmth, welcome – but I was looking for substance, and I wasn't disappointed.

"Listen Matt," he said, leaning in toward me conspiratorially. "I don't buy any of that gatekeeper stuff. You don't need my permission or anyone else's to come and do what you do in London. Eden is called by God to make an impact in this city and in this nation. I want you to be blessed and released to do that and if I can open any doors or make any connections for you then absolutely, I'll do it."

Old and New Connections

In the months following Nims joining the board, another couple of relationships were to develop that would progress us even further toward the goal of becoming a richer network encompassing more varied cultures and heritages. A vicar in North Kensington had approached me to talk about a small and leaderless estate church that fell within his parish, called St Francis. He was concerned that it wasn't thriving and he didn't have the capacity or resources to turn it around. We agreed to bring HTB into the conversation as bringing struggling Anglican churches in London back to life is a central feature of their vision. HTB were fantastic and offered to release and finance one of their bright young curates to pastor the church – his name was Azariah. I'd never met him, or so I thought, so I arranged to meet him for breakfast at a little café near the estate. It was one of those beautiful sunny London mornings and I arrived first, choosing a table on the street outside. As I sipped my cappuccino I was scanning for his arrival. A couple of minutes later I spotted a young black guy wearing a jaunty straw hat strolling around the corner.

"Hang about – I know him!" I thought. "It's my old pal Drew!"

And indeed it was. We'd not seen each other for six or seven years, ever since being involved in a young leaders' programme together with the Billy Graham Association. It turned out he'd begun using his middle name during Bible college, and also developed a hyphenated surname in the process of getting married. I'd been totally fooled by this new identity – but was thrilled to know that such a capable guy was being assigned to the job in the Dalgarno estate. And there was no doubt that his own Caribbean upbringing and family connections would be a tremendous asset in that community.

It had really started to feel like there was an invisible hand guiding Eden's development in London – clearly prayers were being answered, yet I still felt we lacked something. One of the most intimidating aspects of youth and community ministry in London is the presence of street gangs. Again, this isn't necessarily a new thing for Eden to deal with but the scale and ferocity of the problem in London is ratcheted up several notches. I recall being taken on walkabout around several estates in Peckham, estates that had seen more than their fair share of incidents over the years – amongst them the horrific murder of ten-year-old Damilola Taylor in 2000. A few weeks later I read in the newspaper that there'd been a fatal shooting on one of these estates – locally known as 'The Pelican'. My concern was that I felt we needed someone who knew the inside track, perhaps someone whose own story had similarities with those of the teenagers we'd be reaching out to.

At this time we were advertising for a number of Team Leader positions and were beginning to screen and shortlist candidates. Application forms started to arrive from all over the city, and from different parts of the country too. There was one location, however, Tollington, where the shortlist was very short indeed: it only had one name on it. Tollington Parish operates as an inner-city team setup, quite common these days in Anglican circles. Following Sandy's eventual retirement the relationship with Eden passed to

Stu Wright, the associate vicar with primary responsibility toward the ministry in the local community, especially the estates. Stu had already pioneered a number of highly effective ministries that were making a big difference to life in the area, for example a Night Pastors scheme that had made a real dent on the number of reported incidents of antisocial behaviour in the late evening. More than anything though Stu displayed a real passion to affect the youth culture in the area – and especially to offer local youth a real alternative to the gang lifestyle.

We sat together in one of the many Turkish cafes on the Seven Sisters Road taking about how we might build the Eden team, keen to make the most of the foundation already laid. As I always do I shared Eden's deeply held conviction that the right leadership is absolutely key. Stu grinned at me, and I knew straight away that it meant he had someone in mind. He described a rapper he'd worked with on a number of occasions, a very, very good rapper, MOBO award-winning in fact, and yet with his feet firmly on the ground. I was left in no uncertainty that the first thing I needed to do when I had an internet connection was to get onto YouTube and search for 'Jahaziel' – this was the guy we needed, and Stu was confident that if we simply asked him to consider it, God would do the convincing. Some weeks later I had a catch-up call with Stu and although I couldn't see his face this time I knew he was smiling again. Jahaziel had accepted the job offer. Apparently the timing of the move from south of the river to north was just right for him and his young family – his wife and baby daughter.

Don't overlook anyone, by Graham Stevenson

In the enthusiasm of getting Eden Dalgarno started, it was easy to get ahead of ourselves thinking up all the projects we would run, things we would do and services we could offer. But the wisdom of past Eden teams taught us that we needed to put some of the 'doing' on hold and concentrate on 'being'; being present, listening and being out there to get to know our neighbours and neighbourhood. So, the question we initially faced was, how are we going to get to know local people, especially local young people? As we looked out towards partnering with other local youth projects and being out and about on the streets, we almost overlooked the one local young person who was already associated with our small partner church.

Tony had recently turned 16 and had just about given up on the idea of church having anything to offer him. But the arrival of our team of four young(ish!) adults, who are all interested in young people, plus a new minister, Azariah, made sure Tony didn't quietly drift away. Tony got reconnected to the church, but not just coming on Sunday mornings. Eden team member Steve organised a men's curry night and Tony came along for an evening of great food and fun with an 'only in the church' crazy mix of ages, backgrounds and cultures! Steve also helped Tony use his interests and gifts in the church so now it's Tony who'll turn down the microphone if the preacher's going on too long. When Azariah invited Tony along to hear him preach at HTB, Tony experienced a new depth of worship. Tony took the worship even deeper by bringing some estate beats as he beat-boxed through the music set. Tony has continued to grow in his faith and last summer I took Tony along to Soul Survivor, together with the youth group of another church. Tony has since come to our church's first Alpha course and is soaking up all the teaching he can so he can share his faith with friends at school.

Don't get me wrong, we're still looking out for and taking opportunities to get to know local people, especially young people. We're massively grateful to God for opening up the opportunity to be involved in and bless the local community centre, and for all the relationships that are coming out of that. But as well as looking out for young people, we've discovered that in areas like ours there are young people who are ready to start their own journey of discipleship and seem to be just waiting for people to come alongside them and point them to Jesus.

Anonymous Places

When it comes to entering and sharing the struggle of a disadvantaged community one of the things that Eden has always sought to do is to take on the identity of that place within its own name. So for example, our team on a stigmatised council estate called Fitton Hill, in Oldham, is known as Eden Fitton Hill. A few miles down the road there's another Eden team and in exactly the same way, they call themselves Eden Westwood. Incorporating the name of the neighbourhood into the very self-identity of the team has always been an important way of expressing our solidarity with that particular place; it places us within a specific history and living memory.

One thing that took me by surprise in London was the high proportion of anonymous places. On numerous occasions I'd find myself talking to people, locals, resident in the area many years, and they wouldn't actually be able to pin down a name for the place. Usually the best they could come up with would be the name given to the council estate itself, or perhaps the electoral ward. As we reached the stage of actually forming teams in London it really started to give me and Dan Haigh, Eden's Regional Director in London, major headaches. For example, through the initial link with Ric Thorpe we began a close partnership to restart a dying church on the Devon's Road in Tower Hamlets. A fantastic young vicar called Cris Rogers took on the challenge and I recall the two of us having a bizarre conversation. It went a bit like this:

"...well, the Diocese have always called this church All Hallows, Bow," said Cris.

"But are we actually in Bow?" I replied.

"No, not really, the locals think Bow is the area over the other side of the cemetery."

"Isn't this Bromley-by-Bow? I'm sure I heard people at the Housing Office call it that," I asked.

"Yes they do, but it depends who you talk to, they also call it Limehouse sometimes. But really Limehouse is on the other side of the canal, and Bromley-by-Bow is the other side of the DLR."

"So where are we then?"

"I suppose we're just in the Lincoln Estate really – the place doesn't really have another name."

For a Northerner like me it was a bizarre conversation. I'm used to being able to pin down pretty easily where it is that my feet are standing. And this stuff matters, actually. Contemporary regeneration strategy often refers to 'place-making' – well, a pretty fundamental building-block of place is the name it carries. This was by no means the only such conversation that I had on this topic; almost identical discussions took place with our local partners in North Kensington. Here were two neighbourhoods, within a mile of each other, in extremely poor and densely populated patches of inner London that again have little by way of positive self-identity. The Dalgarno estate is built according to the classic 'hide the poor' ethos and the Lancaster West estate is a concrete edifice competing for resources with the insanely chic and expensive districts of Notting Hill and Holland Park.

And so, in naming our first Eden teams in London we simply had to be pragmatic and opt for the name that seemed to fit best, to be most inclusive and affirming of the neighbourhood. Perhaps one day, as we participate in the raising of hopes and the restoring of lives in these places, we'll see God bestowing a new name on them: Hephzibah, and Beulah; "for the Lord will take delight in you, and your land will be married" (*Isaiah 62:4*).

CHAPTER TEN

SENSING A MOVEMENT

I heard the voice of the Lord, saying, Whom shall I send, and who will go for us?
Then said I, Here am I; send me.

Isaiah 6:8

The conditions among the growing underclass in the blighted neighbourhoods of our cities can only be described as desperate. What is needed are charismatic leaders with an inspired alternative vision, along with plans for translating their vision into concrete reality.

Tony Campolo

Outbreak

"We're returning, but not going back."

That was the phrase I'd been using over and over again, every time someone asked about our plans to move back to Salford after two great years in London. We would have loved to have stayed, but it would have been for the wrong reasons, and the last thing I wanted to do was to start getting in the way. Eden was really gaining momentum; the plans that had seemed so flimsy when I first arrived down South had now fleshed out into reality, and all the signs of life were there to be seen. And so here we found ourselves, back up North, sitting on the same old sofas we'd left behind, generally feeling a bit weird and out of place.

Perhaps just to make the situation feel a bit more normal we flicked on the TV, which was already switched to BBC News 24. At the centre of the screen was a dramatic image, a building being slowly swallowed up in a huge fireball. The caption on the screen told us that it was a furniture store in Croydon, South London. The voiceover narrated stories of huge out-of-control mobs on the streets, not just in Croydon but all over the capital. We were dumbstruck by it – it made no sense. Even though we'd been in house-moving mode we'd not failed to see that there had been riots the previous days in Tottenham. I'd spent a bit of time in Tottenham with some really impressive Christians working on the estates up there – so I was already pretty churned up about that. This seemed to be the beginning of something new and even more sinister – this was copycat rioting, and it was clearly spreading fast.

My first thought was "Are our guys OK?" Suddenly London felt a long, long way from Manchester. It was a really strange feeling. Within a few minutes the text messages and phone calls started. One by one I managed to piece together what was going on where, and whether or not any of the estates that we'd moved people into might be in danger. Miraculously they weren't, despite being exactly the sort of places where you'd perhaps expect flashpoints to happen. Whilst searching for breaking news on Twitter I spotted that one of my friends down the road was organising a late-night gathering at his house to pray for peace. I jumped in the car and headed over. It was well past midnight when I got back home but Grace was still waiting up for me. I distinctly remember saying to her as we were getting into bed, "I wonder what it would have felt like if we'd stayed in London a few more days. What will it feel like waking up in London tomorrow?" Well, we didn't need to go to London, because the very next day we found out. The riots travelled north and came to us too.

The newspaper headlines over those days were incredibly revealing. Sensational headlines such as 'Rule of the Mob', 'The Battle for London' and 'Anarchy' were illustrated with images of flaming streets and gangs of hooded youths goading the police. Beneath the headlines something else was happening, something at the same time troubling and revealing. We know that Jesus reserved some of his harshest words for those who demonise and dehumanise others; well this is precisely what rose to the surface in the newspapers as a response to the rioters. Yes, of course there was a collective anger and disgust felt toward those who had acted so selfishly and wreaked such havoc. It seemed, however, that many were happy to act as judge, jury and executioner upon a whole section of society – a so-called 'feral underclass'.

In the times of Jesus there was an Aramaic term of contempt, a swear word, reserved for the most hated and despised. That word was '*Raca*', and it was spoken with a retching of the throat, as if about to spit. Using it publicly could see you in court. The reason that Jesus came down so hard on the demonisers and dehumanisers of his day was because of his vision of the kingdom of heaven. He makes it clear in the Sermon on the Mount that there is absolutely no place for prejudice and bigotry in his new creation. As we look ahead to the future of our inner cities, especially in these austere times, we need to read the signs of the times. It wasn't only the forces of chaos and violence that were unleashed over those crazy few nights in August 2011, a spirit of retching contempt also emerged that doesn't bode well for our society in the years ahead. In every town and city Christians need to remember their calling to be agents of healing and reconciliation, not conspirators in hatred and judgment.

All Points of the Compass

One of the major motivations for chronicling Eden's story through the vehicle of this book is to convey some of the passion and compassion that we feel for young people. If you've been infected with a simmering outrage that merely because some kids happen to live in a dodgy postcode, they're by default excluded from an opportunity to know Jesus, then I don't apologise for that. I also hope that you've come to see the great irony of our age of 'equal opportunity' – that for kids like this the dice are totally loaded toward a secular humanistic narrative of the world. It's a story peddled to them incessantly from every angle – at school, in the music they listen to, from the people they hang out with. In this context the Christian story rarely appears, and if it does then generally in tones of ridicule. Maybe you've caught on to the reality that somebody needs to enter their world in order to bust some stereotypes and build some credibility for the ancient movement once called The Way?

It wasn't long ago that if you wanted to be part of Eden then you'd need to come to Manchester – but those days are behind us now. Whatever part of the country you have a passion for, it's becoming more and more likely that Eden will be developing there soon, if it isn't there already. One of the exciting things about Eden's recent growth is that hope is being born in some of the most unlikely of places. This isn't just about embodying the gospel in really hard places, it's also about embodying the gospel in really forsaken places. Of course the paradox of hope is that to truly be hope then 'the most unlikely of places' is precisely where we ought to expect it to be born. Today, even as you read these lines, hope is being born in the poorly lit alleyways of Eccles, in the cramped kitchens of Fir Vale, on draughty basketball courts in Notting Barns. Hasn't hope always been born in places like this, like smelly animal troughs in Bethlehem?

The North East is becoming a real hive of activity for Eden now. Development of Eden in the region was accelerated by the presence of a vibrant church leaders' network in the city of Newcastle-upon-Tyne. These wonderful women and men of God who call themselves 'Together In Christ' have been meeting together regularly for prayer for over twenty years. Andy and I were given the opportunity to spend some time with them and a really remarkable joining of hearts and vision took place. Following their invitation we began chasing all sorts of local leads in order to begin the process of discerning where the first Eden teams ought to be pioneered. It was a process made more difficult by the geographic spread of the region, and its multiple urban centres – Tyneside, Wearside and Teeside all having their own unique personalities.

After a year or so of under-the-radar research we began building teams in earnest, directing our energy toward three specific communities. The most northerly point of Eden's compass became the coastal town of Blyth, Northumberland; then we looked to Byker, the east end of Newcastle; and finally an overspill council estate called Easterside, a few miles south of Middlesbrough. The work in Easterside was the first to really take off, mainly thanks to the excellent work of team leader Tony Grainge. Sadly the Newcastle work was something of a false-start, although God is clearly doing things in that part of Newcastle that I'm sure will mature and bear fruit in the course of time. The great surprise though was the blossoming of the work in Blyth, which I'll let team-leader and church-planter Phil Sherratt describe in his own words.

On the edge of something big, by Phil Sherratt

After a week of boxing up all we had accumulated in our lives, the big day came. We squeezed everything into a Luton van, including our eight-month-old child, and began our journey of hundreds of miles to pioneer the first Eden in the North East and plant a church in a town that many people don't even know exists. Despite not knowing anyone when we arrived here, God blessed us with a dedicated support network of prayer warriors and we quickly made strong friends.

We made it a priority to connect with local youth and made a point of telling them that we had come to the area because Jesus cared about the community and had sent us. This always provoked a reaction and some great chats! After four months I sensed the time was right for a youth club to be formed. We approached the six young people we knew the best and asked them what a youth group for them might involve. Tina, the most outspoken girl, replied that as Jesus sent us here she would like to know about him, and the others agreed, so we started with a Youth Alpha course. Six girls came, and five found Jesus. Encouraged by the success of the first course we launched a second Youth Alpha and an adult one too. We were overwhelmed when our numbers tipped over 30 and even 40 a time. There is such a spiritual hunger here – I think it has to do with the profound emptiness and isolation that hangs over this place.

Leading an Eden team and starting a church have been, and still are, hugely challenging and frustrating. We have been shocked at the desperate circumstances that some of the young people we meet are dealing with every day – coping with alcoholic parents or being passed on from one foster carer to another. We organised a trip away for some of the youth, just a few days for them to have some fun and enjoy themselves. That's when I discovered that one of the boys in our group had never owned a toothbrush, or even been shown how to use one – and he was eleven years old! Really, that this kind of poverty and neglect exists in twenty-first century Britain is just scandalous.

Eden Blyth continues to be the most extraordinary adventure. There have been times when I've been depressed, stressed and thoroughly fed up, but never once have I doubted that this is where God wants us to be. As a family we have seen God's provision and blessing and we have seen Him move in our lives more than at any other time. We have seen people who have never heard the gospel now encountering the risen Jesus. The power of the gospel continually amazes me when I see how ready people are to respond. We are witnesses to something miraculous that God is doing in this town. He is building His church here, calling His people to live out His love and grace in the lives of the broken, the lost and the least. And we are so privileged to be a part of it.

And Beyond

Looking further ahead, our vision would ultimately be to see Eden playing a part in the transformation of poverty-afflicted communities in all the major British urban centres – including Scotland, Wales and on the other side of the Irish Sea. If the mail in our inbox counts for anything then we can certainly see the stirrings of a missional movement with an emphasis on incarnating the gospel amongst the poor in all corners of the United Kingdom. Personal connections we have in Glasgow, Belfast and Cardiff have also brought a wealth of anecdotal evidence to us about the potential that is waiting to burst out in these great cities.

The immediate concern for Eden is to complete the process we've begun in the North of England, which is to establish the network from coast to coast – from Liverpool in the West to Hull in the East. These great seaport cities are where some of England's most fragile and neglected communities are to be found. Take for example the Preston Road estate in East Hull, the site of our first Humberside team; this neighbourhood of around 3500 people only has a working population of about 1000. In Netherton, the location of our first Eden team in Merseyside, the average annual household income is less than £20,000. We're called to be good news to the poor and they're not going to come to us, so we're going to them. That seems to be the way the Apostle Paul thought about mission, so we're quite happy to simply take a leaf out of his book.

In common then with the many saints down the centuries who

have found themselves gripped by the mission of God, we find ourselves waking up every morning to pursue an implausible and impossible vision – to see the gospel of Jesus work transformation in broken lives and communities. So will the inevitable knocks we take as we chase this dream derail us, send us on a slide into cynicism, a tendency to start making excuses or to begin planning a discreet exit strategy? Well, of course those risks exist, especially when looking at these places and these people through human eyes. That's when it's important to take heed of the dialogue that John records for us in chapter one of his gospel: "Nazareth! Can anything good come from there?" That's right, if the saviour of the world can be brought up in a stigmatised Northern town – and let's not forget that it takes a whole village to raise a child – then maybe there's hope for these places yet. And just in case you're in any doubt, let me introduce you to Nina…

Learning to lead, by Nina Whittaker

I grew up as one of nine kids to a single mum. Mum says not to forget to say that I have a beautiful young mother that raised me! I just kept myself to myself when I first moved to Harpurhey. I can't remember if it was the Eden Bus where I first met the Eden team, or just out and about, but somehow I got invited to the Tuesday club that Eden ran. There I met Andy Smith and he introduced me to the others including Lucy, his wife. Me and Lucy got talking and she invited me to church. I thought, "Really? I've never really done church but I guess I can only give it a go."

One Sunday evening I was telling Lucy about my RE lesson at school; the kids in class had been throwing compasses across the classroom and textbooks out of the window. They tipped all the desks over and it was just really bad. I couldn't work or concentrate at all. I felt really sorry for the teacher too because he was nice and didn't need all that. So then me and Lucy prayed about it, and then Lucy suggested that I pray in the classroom too. I looked at her and was like, "Are you mad? I could get battered if I prayed in the classroom!" but Lucy said that God can hear you even if you pray in your head so I said I'd give it a try.

The following day was my RE lesson, so I sat at the back of the class and started praying. It got weird because as I prayed everything just went totally blank in my head. It was a bit like I had my eyes shut. Like I say, it was dead weird! Before I knew it the bell rang and somehow I'd missed the whole lesson, but I'd done a full page of work and couldn't remember writing it! I showed my teacher and he gave me a merit, a certificate and a bar of chocolate. It was crazy! It could only have been God. That same day after school I went to see Lucy and was laughing when I told her. I wanted to become a Christian and so I gave my life to Jesus there and then on Lucy's doorstep.

Over the next few years the Eden team and home group and Christ Church were really good for me and brought me up to be where I am today.

One day me and my mate Amiee asked our Eden leader, Sid, if he could set up a new group for girls like us. We were shocked when he said 'no'. We were even more shocked when he said, "You're 18 now and I think that you could be leaders, and you could run a session for the younger girls from the estate." We had to take a deep breath because we'd never thought that we could ever be leaders. We went away and started to think about it, and started to get really excited, but we didn't really know what to do or where to start.

So a few days later we went back to Sid to ask him for some advice. He was really good and helped us put together a funding bid to the council. We were successful and they gave us £600 to start a girls' group called 'Shine'. Eden has always welcomed us with arms open wide and we wanted the girls who came to Shine to feel that same kind of welcome. Our vision was to welcome them with open arms and to tell them that we love them and that they are precious and unique. It was important to us to let them know that they could always talk to us about the stuff that's going on in their life.

Amiee and I made a list of younger girls we knew that we thought might need something to do and somebody to talk to. There were nine names on the list and when we invited them they all came. At the beginning some were a bit 'Nah, nah, this is not for me' but they kept coming back every week and we saw them start to progress in their self-esteem and confidence.

It's been an amazing experience and I love how I've grown through it. I have lots of ambitions for the future now. I've looked at joining the army or police, or maybe child care or children's work, but I think the biggest thing for me is to be a youth leader. I would love to have a building that could be a big youth centre. I know it's God who's given me these dreams. Without him I'd not be where I am today.

Mind The Gap

When you finally go ahead and do something a bit crazy and counter-cultural like becoming downwardly mobile you learn a lot about yourself in a short space of time. It's a truth that's borne out time and time again on the Channel 4 TV programme 'The Secret Millionaire'. One of the first things to be discovered is where the lines are drawn in our life. As I mentioned in an earlier chapter, we all have lines in our life; boundaries, defences. But it's a lot more than that too. All of us, through the course of our life, subconsciously construct a set of unwritten rules about who can be close to us and on what conditions. In this way many of us end up in an entirely static relational field. We have certain people in our lives, and we've allowed them a certain amount of access to us, both physically and emotionally. And that's it.

Well, those of us on the original Eden team quickly realised that it was no good relocating ourselves into the neighbourhood if we were just going to retain the barriers in our lives that we'd brought along with us. It was as if we needed to pin up signs on the inside of our front doors reminding us to 'Mind The Gap' as we stepped outside. We urgently needed to redraw our boundaries and we needed an example to look to. The one thing we all had in common was that we had all at some point made a decision to follow Jesus. So it made sense for us to get out our Bibles and start looking at his life in a bit more detail.

The Jesus we met in the gospels was the ultimate barrier-breaker. He's the one of whom John writes, "The Word became flesh and blood and moved into the neighbourhood." In other words, in Christ, God crossed a line, broke through a barrier. By doing this he presented the archetype of missional living; the magnificent poetry of Paul's letter to the Philippians, chapter two, makes that clear enough.

It's worth considering for a moment the world that Jesus entered. Yes, it was the same world we inhabit, a real world of dirt and grass and clouds and rain. But we need to be more specific. Jesus was born into a very particular bit of the world, the Near East, Israel; at a specific time in its history – the Roman Occupation. Life there, and then, probably wasn't much different from the situation in Afghanistan right now. The streets were patrolled by soldiers from a foreign land and the only other authority on the scene was an oppressive, legalistic religious system. First-century Palestine was one of the most divided and regulated societies the world has ever seen. All sorts of rules about men, women, Jews, Gentiles, clean, unclean, what you could or couldn't do, with whom on what day of the week. But Jesus broke the mould. If Jesus could live the way he lived in that time and place, then it speaks volumes into the way we ought to be breaking social conventions and sharing our lives here and now.

Radical Relationality

When we read beyond the gospels of Matthew, Mark, Luke and John, and start reading Paul's letters we can see that this way of life became totally embedded in early Christian life – it's what you might call a 'radical relationality'. The gap between the things that the early church communities claimed to believe, and the way that they actually lived, was tiny, unlike today. It ought to be a no-brainer that as we're restored to right relationship with God we're also challenged to deal with our prejudices, grudges and bitterness towards our fellow human beings. And don't be fooled, that is *the* issue for ministry in deprived urban community. We've found ourselves drawn into the most horrendous relational dysfunction – bitterness, envy, mistrust, hostility, sexual and emotional abuse. That's why there's such an urgent need for followers of Jesus to embody the beliefs they claim to hold so dear. The light conquers the darkness through daily acts of love that prove there's a different way to live.

Paul puts a language around this in his teaching about the 'ministry of reconciliation', which is actually just an echo of the words of Jesus. The past two decades of Eden have convinced me that this must be the central motif for mission in our generation. For an example of how important Jesus considers reconciliation to be, you need look no further than the Sermon on the Mount, immediately following his 'Raca' reference:

"If you are offering your gift at the altar and there remember that your brother has something against you, leave your gift there in front of the altar. First go and be reconciled to your brother; then come and offer your gift." (*Matthew 5:23-24*)

Yes, you heard that right. Jesus says, stop worshipping! Your offering can wait. Go and repair that fracture. Yes, even if it's not your fault!

Why does saying this sound so utterly counter-cultural in our generation? Could it be that we've become so addicted to the mass-produced worship music, and goosebump-oriented meetings and festivals that we've lost sight of the Master's priorities?

As there are precious few pages left in this book I'm going to risk going out on a limb at this point. It would be outrageously arrogant to claim that I know what God desires, but I do feel a bit more confident about suggesting what the world needs. Perhaps they're the same thing?

I think the world needs reconciliation, the deep relational healing that can only be found in the cross and resurrection of Jesus. It's no accident that the symbol of the cross reaches upwards and outwards. Salvation restores us to relationship with the divine and the human, God and neighbour.

What do you think?

Would you agree that Christian mission in our time needs to embody a more radical relationality?

Radical trust.
Radical openness.
Radical love.

Whether you agree or not it's my ardent conviction that only a movement with these values at its heart can break through the barriers that are hemming in disadvantaged young people and families in our nation. Many may dismiss them as dirt, as chavs, as spongers, as not worthy of our time or attention.

Don't let that be you – don't say 'Raca'.

We're all made in God's image.

If this story has persuaded you of anything let it be the reality that some, simply by being born in the wrong postcode on the wrong side of town, are living a life that is a million miles from the abundant, joyful, kingdom life God desires for his children. How you respond to that reality now is up to you. You're free to take a stoic stance, to keep your distance, or you can, perhaps against your natural inclination, let down your defences and allow yourself to be moved.

Of course my hope and prayer is that you'll choose the latter, because until people are moved, there'll never be a movement. Yes, we started out calling Eden a project, then it became known as a network, but its destiny, I believe, is to become a movement…

THE MOVEMENT

Let me ask you a question:

When is a crowd not a crowd?

When is a mass more than merely an audience?

I'd like to venture an answer...

When it unites as a movement.

When it finds purpose and direction.

Yet, until we are moved, there will be no movement.

For every mass-movement begins with a micro-movement

The spark of a synapse,

The twitch of a tendon,

A tightening of the throat and a misting of the eyes...

The origin of a step into the unknown

Best foot forward, a break with the way things are

A statement of future-invoking intent.

Movement hovers and movement broods until its light breaks

like winter dawn over black sea

Movement is a state of being...

Even as a wave exists in its proceeding towards the shore

Even as a flame exists in its flickering

Even as a dance exists in its beat and its rhythm

and the flow of its steps

God exists in Movement

He exists in wave, he exists in flame, he exists in dance

God is a God of movement

He proceeds in a wave of mercy

He flickers with flames of holy passion

He dances in loving, intimate community

He makes his home, his dwelling, amongst us

He is called Immanuel, God with us
Constantly arriving, ever-embracing
This is our God

This is the God who said, 'Whom shall I send? Who will go for me?'
This the God who said, 'Therefore go, into all the world'
This is the God who said 'As the father sent me, so I am sending you'
This is our God...
...the God at the head of the movement,
The first into the fray
The first-born from amongst the dead
Yes, even the creeping rigor mortis of the grave
Was vanquished by his anastasis, the resurrection
The moment that kinetic triumphed over static
Life took victory over death
Come on!

And you were made for movement
You were made to participate in this movement of God
This is what you were born for
You were not born to live a small, ordinary life
of safe boundaries, tidy fences, you were made for more...
You were made to go, to journey,
To become the vanguard of God's purposes in this generation
To go to the forgotten places
To go to the forsaken
To be a herald, to be a witness, to be a prophet
To be a friend... of the lost and the last and the least
You are more than a face in a crowd,
You belong to the mission of God,
You were born to be part of the movement.

AFTERWORD

As the pages of this book make clear, Eden has been pursuing a simple God-given vision of streams in the wasteland. The vision remains the same today, it's just that the canvas onto which that vision is cast seems to grow larger and larger. Soon the Eden Network will have a presence in all of the major urban centres in England. Beyond that there have also been early conversations about how we might begin to extend throughout the rest of the British Isles too. After all, what's so special about England? Surely envisioned people in Wales, Scotland and Ireland ought to be able to develop Eden teams of their own?

Our prayer and longing now is for Eden to experience true multiplication. That means that extending into Europe is also a very real possibility, as well as more far-flung continents such as North and South America, Australasia and Africa. Our only limitation is that we sense that God told us to 'Give it away' not 'Throw it away'.

Considering these future possibilities it's obvious that the way Eden operates needs to continue to evolve. Even with our growth accelerating we'll never have the resources of prayer, pounds and people to plant a full-blown Eden into every deprived neighbourhood. So if we can't go faster, can we get smarter? Maybe there's another way we can do this? All the evidence suggests that there are plenty of passionate Jesus-followers out there who want to make a difference in challenging communities. We receive emails from such people just about every week. The problem so far has been that many of them don't fit our tight criteria for partnership; for instance they aren't within one of the large urban centres where we have a Regional Hub or they may not feel called to have the same priority towards youth that we do.

Our concern is that when we say 'no' to these people (which may be you!) one of two things may happen, neither of which is positive. Either a) there's an onset of inertia, a lack of confidence to step out without an organisation like us supporting; or b) they have a go anyway, lacking awareness and experience of the issues, and things get messy. Therefore, after a lot of thought and prayer we've devised a new way that churches and other Christian groups can relate to the Eden Network, and we're calling it the 'Associates' scheme. By establishing an Eden Associates network the plan is to see:

- More Christian groups confidently stepping out to make a difference in communities, and
- More Christian groups establishing high-quality ministries that are fruitful and sustainable

We also believe that we are called to be generous as God has been generous to us. We've made lots of mistakes, learned lots of lessons and have lots to share in terms of seeing breakthrough in these tough communities. If we were to define a Big Hairy Audacious Goal for Eden Associates it might look a bit like this:

"A Missional Community bringing about transformation in every poverty-afflicted neighbourhood in ~~Britain~~ ~~Europe~~ the world!"

If you like the sound of that and you think that you'd like to become an Associate team within the wider Eden family then we'd love to hear from you. You can drop us a line at the following email address: **associates@eden-network.org**

Thanks, and do keep praying for Eden.

Andy Hawthorne OBE

Chief Executive, The Message Trust

EDEN'S FIVE CORNERSTONES

We are rooted in a local church

Rooted in a supportive local church we seek to positively impact our community by the consistent witness of our presence and our proclamation. We desire to be a blessing to, and enjoy fellowship with, the whole body of Christ.

We are focused on the toughest neighbourhoods

That is, communities widely recognised as suffering from multiple deprivations, such as: high crime, poor health, low educational achievement, dilapidated environment, broken families and few opportunities for young people.

A large team of people establish their homes in the heart of the community

Devoted individuals with a recognised calling to live an incarnational lifestyle of integrating with the community. Dozens of such people join together in a missional team dynamic and make themselves available long-term for the benefit of their community.

Our first priority is reaching youth to see their full potential unlocked

Young people of high school age are seen to be a key part of the transformation of the whole neighbourhood. Our goal is to help them to achieve all their God-given potential, introducing them to Jesus by creating repeated and varied opportunities for them to hear, experience and respond to the gospel.

We belong to a wider relational network

As teams called to a variety of locations we recognise the need to make time to gather together periodically to share our stories and experiences, work through issues and challenges, and offer support and encouragement to one another.

EDEN'S FIVE DISTINCTIVES

We are incarnational

We are devoted to the communities that we have adopted as home. This is far more than simply being a good neighbour or even being a willing local volunteer. We have a sense of calling and commitment to live long-term as salt and light, fleshing out the grace of God.

We are relational

Relationships are the currency of our lives and the primary route through which transformation takes place. Therefore we choose to lead an authentic, open life within an accountable team dynamic. This way of life may be expressed in many ways such as valuing family, practising hospitality and loving the unlovely.

We are purposeful

We are not passive observers in our communities, we are there to be a deliberate witness of Jesus Christ. The church we belong to has an overarching mission which recognises the synergy between who we are and what we do. In times of excitement and times of endurance we will retain our redemptive intent.

We are countercultural

Whilst acknowledging the importance of embracing the culture we live in we will retain a deliberately different stance on issues of integrity and morality as Jesus has taught us. We expect challenges as we model sacrificial living as urban missionaries who desire to know Jesus and make him known.

We are holistic

Our conviction is that God cares for whole people – not just souls. We see clearly in the Bible that the people of God are expected to play an active role in his grand restoration plan. In practice this will mean that we will develop innovative responses meeting a wide range of relational, recreational, educational, emotional and spiritual needs.

OTHER GREAT BOOKS

ANDY HAWTHORNE
HOPE UNLEASHED

What has washing someone's car got to do with the gospel?

Committed to bringing the Christian message to young people in his hometown of Manchester, England, Andy Hawthorne was shocked when a missions partner told him he shouldn't just preach the gospel but also engage in community projects.

And it got him thinking: what, exactly, should the priority of the church be? Should it be the lamp on a stand - bold, unashamed gospel proclamation to as many as possible? Or should it be more salt and yeast – serving and blessing the vulnerable and the marginalized, with no questions asked?

The answer, of course, is both. Christians who truly want to follow Jesus should explain the good news with words - but also make sure to demonstrate the gospel through what's been described as random acts of kindness. Written in a warm, passionate, nonreligious style, Hope Unleashed is filled with moving true stories and practical ideas and strategies for Christian mission based on word and deed.

ANDY HAWTHORNE
DIARY OF A DANGEROUS VISION

This is the story of one man's conversion and the blossoming of an ever-growing group of Christians set to take Christ into the most demanding and tough urban areas.

Their vision spawned a number of different related initiatives: the beginning and growth of the World Wide Message Tribe, Cameron Dante's conversion, and the Eden project in Manchester.

Andy Hawthorne was born in Manchester and rebelled as a teenager before being brought to Christ by his brother, Simon. They started a fashion business and it was some of the youths who they employed that inspired Andy to organise Message to schools, the work of the World Wide Message Tribe and Eden.

'A bunch of ordinary people with the fire of an extraordinary God burning in them.' J John

ANDY HAWTHORNE
THE MESSAGE 20
CELEBRATING TWO DECADES OF CHANGED LIVES

In 2012, The Message celebrates 20 years of working with young people in Greater Manchester. Starting from one schools band in 1992, our work has expanded to reach young people in schools, communities and prisons in the North West and beyond. Thousands of lives have been changed as God has worked through our teams.

To mark this exciting milestone in our history we are publishing a lavish 20th Anniversary hardback book with a new history written by Andy Hawthorne and dozens of moving stories and testimonies from people who have shared the journey with us.

Facebook.com/EdenNetwork

OR VISIT OUR WEBSITE AT:

www.eden-network.org

MAKING A GIFT TO EDEN

PLEASE FILL IN THIS FORM AND RETURN TO:

Eden Network, Lancaster House, Harper Road, Sharston, Manchester, M22 4RG

NAME(S)

ADDRESS

POSTCODE

TEL

EMAIL

IF YOU ARE ABLE PLEASE **GIVE REGULARLY**

New Regular Gift ☐   Increase my Current Giving ☐ (please tick)

I/We would like my/our monthly gift to be:

£6 ☐   **£13** ☐   **£20** ☐   Or £ ☐☐☐☐☐☐ . ☐☐

To be collected on **15th** ☐ or **28th** ☐ of the month
(please tick)

Starting on D D M M Y Y

DIRECT Debit

PLEASE NOW COMPLETE THE DIRECT DEBIT INSTRUCTION ON THE NEXT PAGE

Using Direct Debits makes life easier for us but if you'd prefer to give via

Standing Order, please contact our Supporter Relations Team on:

0161 946 2300

ALTERNATIVELY, PLEASE **GIVE A ONE-OFF GIFT**

Cheque £ ☐☐☐☐☐ . ☐☐ Payable to "The Message Trust"

Card £ ☐☐☐☐☐ . ☐☐ We accept the following: **VISA** MasterCard Maestro SOLO

Card No. ☐☐☐☐ ☐☐☐☐ ☐☐☐☐ ☐☐☐☐

Start M M Y Y Exp M M Y Y   CSC ☐☐☐ Issue No. ☐☐
REQUIRED
(Last 3 digits on signature strip)

Source Code: APP11000

Signature [ ]   Start M M Y Y

YOU CAN ALSO CALL TO:

Set up a **new** regular gift,
change your address details
or **ask** to recieve our regular mailings
by calling our Supporter Relations Team
on **0161 946 2300**

giftaid it

**Don't forget to
Gift Aid your donation
on the next page**

 *giftaid it*

I would like The Message to treat all donations I have made in the last four years, and all future donations, as Gift Aid donations until I notify otherwise.

Signature [   ]

Date [D][D][M][M][Y][Y]

You must pay an amount of income tax at least equal to the tax which The Message reclaims on your donation. If your circumstances change in the future and this is no longer the case, you must cancel your declaration by notifying us in writing.
Please notify The Message Trust if you change your name or address.

 DIRECT Debit

Instruction to your bank or building society to pay by Direct Debit

Please fill in the whole form using a ball point pen and send it to:

The Message Trust, Lancaster House, Harper Road, Sharston, Manchester, M22 4RG

Service User Number

| 6 | 8 | 8 | 9 | 6 | 4 |

Name and full postal address of your bank or building society

To: The Manager	Bank/Building Society
Address	
	Postcode

Instruction to your bank or building society

Please pay The Message Trust Direct Debits from the account detailed in this Instruction subject to the safeguards assured by the Direct Debit Guarantee. I understand that this Instruction may remain with The Message Trust and, if so, details will be passed electronically to my bank/building society.

Name(s) of account holder(s)

| |
| |

Bank/building society account number

| | | | | | | | |

Branch Sort Code

| | | | - | | | - | | |

Signatures

| |

Date

| |

Banks and building societies may not accept Direct Debit Instructions for some types of account

- -

MAKING A GIFT TO EDEN

PLEASE FILL IN THIS FORM AND RETURN TO:

Eden Network, Lancaster House, Harper Road, Sharston, Manchester, M22 4RG

NAME(S)

ADDRESS

POSTCODE

TEL

EMAIL

IF YOU ARE ABLE PLEASE **GIVE REGULARLY**

New Regular Gift ☐   Increase my Current Giving ☐ (please tick)

I/We would like my/our monthly gift to be:

£6 ☐   **£13** ☐   **£20** ☐   Or £ ☐☐☐☐☐ . ☐☐

To be collected on **15th** ☐ or **28th** ☐ of the month (please tick)

Starting on ☐D☐D☐M☐M☐Y☐Y

DIRECT Debit

PLEASE NOW COMPLETE THE DIRECT DEBIT INSTRUCTION ON THE NEXT PAGE

Using Direct Debits makes life easier for us but if you'd prefer to give via

Standing Order, please contact our Supporter Relations Team on:

0161 946 2300

ALTERNATIVELY, PLEASE **GIVE A ONE-OFF GIFT**

Cheque £ ☐☐☐☐☐ . ☐☐ Payable to "The Message Trust"

Card £ ☐☐☐☐☐ . ☐☐ We accept the following: **VISA** MasterCard Maestro SOLO

Card No. ☐☐☐☐ ☐☐☐☐ ☐☐☐☐ ☐☐☐☐

Start ☐M☐M☐Y☐Y Exp ☐M☐M☐Y☐Y CSC ☐☐☐ Issue No. ☐☐

REQUIRED
(Last 3 digits on signature strip)

Source Code: APP11000

Signature ☐   Start ☐M☐M☐Y☐Y

YOU CAN ALSO CALL TO:

Set up a **new** regular gift,
change your address details
or **ask** to recieve our regular mailings
by calling our Supporter Relations Team
on **0161 946 2300**

giftaid it

**Don't forget to
Gift Aid your donation
on the next page**

Reg Charity No. 1081467

 I would like The Message to treat all donations I have made in the last four years, and all future donations, as Gift Aid donations until I notify otherwise.

Signature _____

Date D D M M Y Y

You must pay an amount of income tax at least equal to the tax which The Message reclaims on your donation. If your circumstances change in the future and this is no longer the case, you must cancel your declaration by notifying us in writing.
Please notify The Message Trust if you change your name or address.

 DIRECT Debit

Instruction to your bank or building society to pay by Direct Debit

Please fill in the whole form using a ball point pen and send it to:

The Message Trust, Lancaster House,
Harper Road, Sharston, Manchester, M22 4RG

Service User Number

`6 8 8 9 6 4`

Name and full postal address of your bank or building society

To: The Manager _____ Bank/Building Society

Address _____

_____

Postcode _____

Instruction to your bank or building society

Please pay The Message Trust Direct Debits from the account detailed in this Instruction subject to the safeguards assured by the Direct Debit Guarantee. I understand that this Instruction may remain with The Message Trust and, if so, details will be passed electronically to my bank/building society.

Name(s) of account holder(s)

_____

_____

Bank/building society account number

☐☐☐☐☐☐☐☐

Branch Sort Code

☐☐ ☐☐ ☐☐

Signatures

_____

Date

_____

FOR THE MESSAGE TRUST OFFCIAL USE ONLY: This is not part of the instruction to your bank or building society.		
DATE RECEIVED	GAD	SER No.
DEST	PLG/REF	

Banks and building societies may not accept Direct Debit Instructions for some types of account

- -

The Direct Debit Guarantee

This guarantee should be detached and retained by the payer

 DIRECT Debit

- This Guarantee is offered by all banks and building societies that accept instructions to pay Direct Debits
- If there are any changes to the amount, date or frequency of your Direct Debit The Message Trust will notify you 10 working days in advance of your account being debited or as otherwise agreed. If you request The Message Trust to collect a payment, confirmation of the amount and date will be given to you at the time of the request

- If an error is made in the payment of your Direct Debit, by The Message Trust or your bank or building society you are entitled to a full and immediate refund of the amount paid from your bank or building society when The Message Trust asks you to
 – if you receive a refund you are not entitled to, you must pay it back
- You can cancel a Direct Debit at any time by simply contacting your bank or building society. Written confirmation may be required. Please also notify us.

About the author

Matt Wilson has been involved in Eden's work since its inception. He been its Director for the last ten years. Matt also serves on the leadership team of Eden's parent charity – The Message Trust, a youth and community ministry based in Manchester, England.

Over 20 years The Message has forged a reputation for being one of the most innovative youth ministries in Europe pioneering in areas of music, media, urban ministry and large-scale mission mobilisation.

Matt came into vocational ministry from a career background in the advertising industry and has since gone on to study master's degrees in management and in theology.

He lives in Salford with his wife Grace and two young sons, Izzy and JJ.

You can follow Matt on Twitter
@mattwi1s0n